ITALIAN RECIPES 2022

DELICIOUS MEALS FOR EATING WELL EVERYDAY

FOR BEGINNERS

MIKE ROSSI

FORZA ITALIA!

TABLE OF CONTENTS

Baked Onions 10

Onions with Balsamic Vinegar 12

Red Onion Confit 14

Roasted Onion and Beet Salad 16

Pearl Onions with Honey and Orange 18

Peas with Onions 20

Peas with Prosciutto and Green Onions 22

Sweet Peas with Lettuce and Mint 24

Easter Pea Salad 25

Roasted Peppers 27

Roasted Pepper Salad 29

Roasted Peppers with Onions and Herbs 30

Baked Peppers with Tomatoes 32

Peppers with Balsamic Vinegar 34

Pickled Peppers 36

Peppers with Almonds 38

Peppers with Tomatoes and Onions 40

Stuffed Frying Peppers 42

Neapolitan-Style Stuffed Peppers 44

Stuffed Peppers, Ada Boni's Style 47

Fried Peppers 49

Sautéed Peppers with Zucchini and Mint 51

Roasted Pepper and Eggplant Terrine 53

Sweet-and-Sour Potatoes 56

Potatoes with Balsamic Vinegar 58

Venetian-Style Potatoes 60

"Jumped" Potatoes 62

Potato-Pepper Sauté 64

Mashed Potatoes with Parsley and Garlic 66

Herbed New Potatoes with Pancetta 68

Potatoes with Tomatoes and Onions 70

Roasted Potatoes with Garlic and Rosemary 72

Roasted Potatoes with Mushrooms 74

Potatoes and Cauliflower, Basilicata Style 76

Potatoes and Cabbage in the Pan 78

Potato and Spinach Torte 80

Neapolitan Potato Croquettes 83

Dad's Neapolitan Potato Pie 86

Skillet Tomatoes 89

Steamed Tomatoes 90

Baked Tomatoes 91

Tomatoes Stuffed with Farro 93

Roman Stuffed Tomatoes 95

Roasted Tomatoes with Balsamic Vinegar 97

Zucchini Carpaccio 99

Zucchini with Garlic and Mint 101

Sautéed Zucchini 103

Zucchini with Prosciutto 105

Zucchini with Parmesan Crumbs 107

Zucchini Gratin 109

Zucchini with Tomatoes and Anchovies 111

Zucchini Stew 113

Abruzzo-Style Almond Cake with Chocolate Frosting 115

Rum and Currant Loaf Cakes 118

Warm Amaretti Cakes 121

Marsala Walnut Cake 124

Crunchy Walnut Cake 126

Piedmontese Hazelnut Cake 128

Mantua Cake 130

Christmas Sweet Bread 132

Chocolate-Raisin Bread Pudding 135

Panettone Bread Pudding 137

Biscotti Bread Pudding 139

Pear and Apple Cake 141

Single-Crust Pastry 143

Double-Crust Pastry 145

Berry Mascarpone Tart 147

Summer Fruit Tart 150

Blueberry Crostata 152

Raspberry Cream Tart 155

Sour-Cherry Jam Tart 158

Apple Marzipan Tart 160

Fig and Walnut Crostata 164

Dried Fig Tart 168

Lemon Almond Tart 171

Almond and Peach Tart 174

Pine Nut Tart 177

Winter Fruit and Nut Crostata 180

Ricotta Lattice Tart 183

Roman Ricotta Tart 186

Ricotta Jam Tart 189

Chocolate Tart 191

Rice Pudding Tart 193

Cornmeal Berry Tart 196

Spice and Nut Tart 200

Cinnamon Plum Torte 203

Cannoli Cream 207

Chocolate Cannoli Cream 209

Pastry Cream 210

Cream Puffs 212

St. Joseph's Fritters 215

Baked Onions

Cipolle al Forno

Makes 4 to 8 servings

These onions turn smooth and sweet when cooked; try them with roast beef.

4 medium white or red onions, peeled

½ cup plain dry bread crumbs

¼ cup freshly grated Parmigiano-Reggiano or Pecorino Romano

2 tablespoons olive oil

Salt and freshly ground black pepper

1. Bring a medium saucepan of water to a boil. Add the onions and reduce the heat so that the water just simmers. Cook 5 minutes. Let the onions cool in the water in the pan. Drain the onions and cut them in half crosswise.

2. Place a rack in the center of the oven. Preheat the oven to 350°F. Oil a baking pan just large enough to hold the onions in a single layer. Place the onions in the pan cut-side up. In a small bowl,

mix together the bread crumbs, cheese, olive oil, and salt and pepper to taste. Spoon the bread crumbs on top of the onions.

3. Bake 1 hour or until the onions are golden and tender when pierced with a knife. Serve hot or at room temperature.

Onions with Balsamic Vinegar

Cipolle al Balsamico

Makes 6 servings

Balsamic vinegar complements the sweet flavor and color of red onions. These go well with roast pork or pork chops.

6 medium red onions

6 tablespoons extra-virgin olive oil

3 tablespoons balsamic vinegar

Salt and freshly ground black pepper

1. Place a rack in the center of the oven. Preheat the oven to 375°F. Line a baking pan with foil.

2. Wash the onions, but do not peel them. Place the onions in the prepared pan. Bake the onions 1 hour to $1^{1}/_{2}$ hours, until tender when pierced with a knife.

3. Trim off the root ends of the onions and peel off the skin. Cut the onions into quarters and place them in a bowl. Add the oil,

vinegar, and salt and pepper to taste, and toss to combine. Serve hot or at room temperature.

Red Onion Confit

Confettura di Cipolle Rosse

Makes about 1 pint

Tropea, on the Calabrian coast, is known for its sweet red onions. Though the red onions in the United States are more pungent, you can still make this delicious jam that we ate at Locanda di Alia in Castrovillari. The jam was served with golden fried sardines, but it is also good with pork chops or grilled chicken. I also like it as a condiment with a sharp cheese, such as aged pecorino.

A variation of the jam includes some chopped fresh mint. Be sure to use a heavy-bottomed saucepan and keep the heat very low to prevent the onions from sticking. Add a little water if they dry out too quickly.

1¼ pounds red onions, very finely chopped

1 cup dry red wine

1 teaspoon salt

2 tablespons unsalted butter

1 tablespoon balsamic vinegar

1 or 2 tablespoons honey

About 1 tablespoon sugar

1. In a medium heavy saucepan, combine the onions, red wine, and salt over medium heat. Bring to a simmer and turn the heat to low. Cover and cook, stirring often, for 1 hour 15 minutes or until the onions are very tender. The onions will be slightly translucent.

2. Stir in the butter, balsamic vinegar, and 1 tablespoon each of the honey and sugar. Cook uncovered, stirring often, until all of the liquid has evaporated and the mixture is very thick.

3. Let cool slightly. Serve at room temperature or slightly warm. This keeps in the refrigerator for up to a month. To reheat, place the confit in a small bowl set over a pan of simmering water, or warm it in a microwave.

Roasted Onion and Beet Salad

Insalata di Cipolla e Barbabietola

Makes 6 servings

If you have never had fresh beets in season, you really should try them. When they are young and tender, they are remarkably sweet and flavorful. Buy them in the summer and fall, when they are at their best. As they age they become woody and tasteless.

6 beets, trimmed and scrubbed

2 large onions, peeled

6 tablespoons olive oil

2 tablespoons red wine vinegar

Salt and freshly ground black pepper

6 fresh basil leaves

1. Place a rack in the center of the oven. Preheat the oven to 400°F. Scrub the beets and wrap them in a large sheet of aluminum foil, sealing tightly. Place the package on a baking sheet.

2. Cut the onions into bite-size pieces. Place them in a baking pan and toss with 2 tablespoons of the olive oil.

3. Place the package of beets and the pan of onions side by side in the oven. Bake 1 hour or until the beets are tender when pierced with a knife and the onions are browned.

4. Let the beets cool. Peel off the skins and cut the beets into wedges.

5. In a large bowl, toss the beets and onions with 1/4 cup olive oil, the vinegar, and salt and pepper to taste. Sprinkle with the basil and serve immediately.

Pearl Onions with Honey and Orange

Cipolline Profumate all'Arancia

Makes 8 servings

Sweet and tart pearl onions flavored with honey, orange, and vinegar are good with a holiday turkey or capon, roast pork, or as an appetizer with sliced salumi. You can make them ahead, but they should be reheated gently before serving.

2 pounds pearl onions

1 navel orange

2 tablespoons unsalted butter

¼ cup honey

¼ cup white wine vinegar

Salt and freshly ground black pepper

1. Bring a large pot of water to a boil. Add the onions and cook for 3 minutes. Drain and cool them under running water. With a sharp paring knife, shave off the tip of the root ends. Do not slice off the ends too deeply or the onions will fall apart during cooking. Slip off the skins.

2. With a swivel-blade vegetable peeler, remove the orange zest. Stack the strips of zest and cut them into thin matchsticks. Squeeze the juice from the orange. Set aside.

3. In a large skillet, melt the butter over medium heat. Add the onions and cook 30 minutes or until lightly browned, shaking the pan occasionally so that they do not stick.

4. Add the orange juice, zest, honey, vinegar, and salt and pepper to taste. Turn the heat to low and cook 10 minutes, turning the onions frequently, until the onions are tender when pierced with a knfe and glazed with the sauce. Let cool slightly. Serve warm.

Peas with Onions

Piselli con Cipolle

Makes 4 servings

A little water added to the pan helps the onion to mellow and soften without browning. The sweetness of the onion enhances the flavor of the peas.

2 tablespoons olive oil

1 medium onion, finely chopped

4 tablespoons water

2 cups fresh shelled peas or 1 (10-ounce) package frozen peas

Pinch of dried oregano

Salt

1. Pour the oil into a medium saucepan. Add the onion and 2 tablespoons of the water. Cook, stirring frequently, until the onion is very tender, about 15 minutes.

2. Stir in the peas, the remaining 2 tablespoons of water, the oregano, and the salt. Cover and cook until the peas are tender, 5 to 10 minutes.

Peas with Prosciutto and Green Onions

Piselli al Prosciutto

Makes 4 servings

These peas are good with lamb chops or roast lamb.

3 tablespoons unsalted butter

4 green onions, trimmed and thinly sliced

2 cups fresh shelled peas or 1 (10-ounce) package frozen peas

1 teaspoon sugar

Salt

4 thin slices imported Italian prosciutto, cut crosswise into thin strips

1. Melt 2 tablespoons of the butter in a medium skillet. Add the green onions and cook 1 minute.

2. Add the peas, sugar, and salt to taste. Stir in 2 tablespoons water and cover the pan. Cook over low heat until the peas are tender, 5 to 10 minutes.

3. Stir in the prosciutto and remaining 1 tablespoon of butter. Cook 1 minute more and serve hot.

Sweet Peas with Lettuce and Mint

Piselli alla Menta

Makes 4 servings

Even frozen peas taste like fresh-picked when they are prepared this way. The lettuce adds a slight crunch and the mint a bright, fresh flavor.

2 tablespoons unsalted butter

¼ cup onion, very finely chopped

2 cups fresh shelled peas or 1 (10-ounce) package frozen peas

1 cup shredded lettuce leaves

12 mint leaves, torn into bits

Salt and freshly ground black pepper

1. In a medium saucepan, melt the butter over medium heat. Add the onion and cook until tender and golden, about 10 minutes.

2. Add the peas, lettuce, mint leaves, and salt and pepper to taste. Stir in 2 tablespoons water and cover the pan. Cook 5 to 10 minutes or until the peas are tender. Serve hot.

Easter Pea Salad

Insalata di Pasqua

Makes 4 servings

In the 1950s Romeo Salta was considered one of the best Italian restaurants in New York City. It stood out because it was very elegant and served northern Italian food at a time when most people were only familiar with family-style restaurants serving the red sauced dishes of the south. The owner, Romeo Salta, had learned the restaurant business by working on luxury cruise liners—at that time, the finest training ground for restaurant personnel. This salad would appear on the menu around Easter, when fresh peas became abundant. The original recipe also contained anchovies, though I prefer the salad without them. Sometimes I add chopped Swiss or a similar cheese along with the prosciutto.

2½ cups fresh shelled peas or 1 (10-ounce) package frozen peas

Salt

1 hard-cooked egg yolk

¼ cup olive oil

¼ cup lemon juice

Freshly ground black pepper

2 ounces sliced imported Italian prosciutto, cut crosswise into narrow strips

1. For either fresh or frozen peas, bring a medium saucepan of water to boiling. Add the peas and salt to taste. Cook until the peas are barely tender, about 3 minutes. Drain the peas. Cool them under cold running water. Blot the peas dry.

2. In a serving bowl, mash the egg yolk with a fork. Whisk in the oil, lemon juice, and salt and pepper to taste. Add the peas and toss gently. Add the prosciutto strips and serve immediately.

Roasted Peppers

Peperoni Arrostiti

Makes 8 servings

Roasted peppers are good in salads, omelets, and sandwiches. They freeze well, too, so you can make a batch in the summer when peppers are plentiful and keep them for winter meals.

8 large red, yellow, or green bell peppers

1. Cover the broiler pan with foil. Place the broiler pan about 3 inches away from the heat source. Place the whole peppers on the pan. Turn on the broiler to high. Broil the peppers, turning them frequently with tongs, about 15 minutes or until the skin blisters and they are charred all over. Put the peppers in a bowl. Cover with foil and let cool.

2. Cut the peppers in half, draining the juices into a bowl. Peel off the skins and discard the seeds and stems.

3. Cut the peppers lengthwise into 1-inch strips and place them in a serving bowl. Strain the juices over the peppers.

4. Serve at room temperature or store in the refrigerator and serve chilled. The peppers keep 3 days in the refrigerator or 3 months in the freezer.

Roasted Pepper Salad

Insalata di Peperoni Arrostiti

Makes 8 servings

Serve these peppers as part of an antipasto assortment, as a side dish with grilled tuna or pork, or as an antipasto with sliced fresh mozzarella.

1 recipe (8 peppers) Roasted Peppers

1/3 cup extra-virgin olive oil

4 basil leaves, torn into bits

2 garlic cloves, thinly sliced

Salt and freshly ground black pepper

Prepare the peppers, if necessary. Toss the peppers with the oil, basil, garlic, and salt and pepper to taste. Let stand 1 hour before serving.

Roasted Peppers with Onions and Herbs

Peperoni Arrostiti con Cipolle

Makes 4 servings

Serve these peppers hot or at room temperature. They also make a good topping for crostini.

½ recipe Roasted Peppers; use red or yellow bell peppers

1 medium onion, halved and thinly sliced

Pinch of crushed red pepper

2 tablespoons olive oil

Salt

½ teaspoon dried oregano, crumbled

2 tablespoons chopped fresh flat-leaf parsley

1. Prepare the peppers through step 3, if necessary. Then, drain the peppers and cut them lengthwise into $1/2$-inch strips.

2. In a medium skillet, cook the onion with the crushed red pepper in the oil over medium heat until the onion is tender and golden, about 10 minutes. Add the peppers, oregano, and salt to taste. Cook, stirring occasionally, until heated through, about 5 minutes. Stir in the parsley and cook 1 minute more. Serve hot or at room temperature.

Baked Peppers with Tomatoes

Peperoni al Forno

Makes 4 servings

In this recipe from Abruzzo, a fresh, not-too-hot chile seasons the bell peppers. Crushed red pepper or a small dried chile pepper can be substituted. These peppers are good in a sandwich.

2 large red bell peppers

2 large yellow bell peppers

1 chile, such as jalapeño, seeded and chopped

3 tablespoons olive oil

Salt

2 garlic cloves, chopped

2 medium tomatoes, peeled, seeded, and chopped

1. Place a rack in the center of the oven. Preheat the oven to 400°F. Oil a large baking pan. Stand the peppers on a cutting board. Holding the stem in one hand, place the cutting edge of a large heavy chef's knife just beyond the edge of the cap. Cut straight down. Turn the pepper 90° and cut straight down again. Repeat, turning and cutting the remaining two sides. Discard the core, seeds, and stem, which will be in one piece. Cut away any membranes and scrape out any seeds.

2. Cut the peppers lengthwise into 1-inch strips. Add the chile to the pan. Add the oil and salt to taste and toss well. Spread the peppers out in the pan.

3. Bake the peppers 25 minutes. Add the garlic and tomatoes and stir well. Bake 20 minutes more or until the peppers are tender when pierced with a knife. Serve hot.

Peppers with Balsamic Vinegar

Peperoni al Balsamico

Makes 6 servings

The sweetness of balsamic vinegar complements the sweetness of peppers. Serve these hot with pork or lamb chops or at room temperature with cold chicken or roast pork.

6 large red bell peppers

¼ cup olive oil

Salt and freshly ground black pepper

2 tablespoons balsamic vinegar

1. Place a rack in the center of the oven. Preheat the oven to 400°F. Stand the peppers on a cutting board. Holding the stem in one hand, place the cutting edge of a large heavy chef's knife just beyond the edge of the cap. Cut straight down. Turn the pepper 90° and cut straight down again. Repeat, turning and cutting the remaining two sides. Discard the core, seeds, and stem, which will be in one piece. Cut away any membranes and scrape out any seeds.

2. Cut the peppers into 1-inch strips. Place them in a large shallow roasting pan with the oil and salt and pepper. Toss well. Bake the peppers 30 minutes.

3. Stir in the vinegar. Bake the peppers 20 minutes more or until tender. Serve hot or at room temperature.

Pickled Peppers

Peperoni Sott'Aceto

Makes 2 pints

Colorful peppers packed in vinegar are delicious in sandwiches or with cold meats. These can be used to make the Molise-Style Pepper Sauce.

2 large red bell peppers

2 large yellow bell peppers

Salt

2 cups white wine vinegar

2 cups water

Pinch of crushed red pepper

1. Stand the peppers on a cutting board. Holding the stem in one hand, place the cutting edge of a large heavy chef's knife just beyond the edge of the cap. Cut straight down. Turn the pepper 90° and cut straight down again. Repeat, turning and cutting the remaining two sides. Discard the core, seeds, and stem, which will be in one piece. Cut away any membranes and scrape out any seeds. Cut the peppers lengthwise into 1-inch strips. Place the peppers in a colander set over a plate and sprinkle with salt. Let stand 1 hour to drain.

2. In a nonreactive saucepan, combine the vinegar, water, and crushed red pepper. Bring to a simmer. Remove from the heat and let cool slightly.

3. Rinse the bell peppers under cold water and pat them dry. Pack the peppers in 2 sterilized pint jars. Pour on the cooled vinegar mixture and seal. Let stand in a cool, dark place 1 week before using.

Peppers with Almonds

Peperoni alle Mandorle

Makes 4 servings

An old friend of my mother's whose family came from Ischia, a small island in the bay of Naples, gave her this recipe. She liked to serve it for lunch over slices of Italian bread fried in olive oil until golden.

2 red and 2 yellow bell peppers

1 garlic clove, lightly crushed

3 tablespoons olive oil

2 medium tomatoes, peeled, seeded, and chopped

¼ cup water

2 tablespoons capers

4 anchovy fillets, chopped

4 ounces toasted almonds, coarsely chopped

1. Stand the peppers on a cutting board. Holding the stem in one hand, place the cutting edge of a large heavy chef's knife just beyond the edge of the cap. Cut straight down. Turn the pepper 90° and cut straight down again. Repeat, turning and cutting the remaining two sides. Discard the core, seeds, and stem, which will be in one piece. Cut away any membranes and scrape out any seeds.

2. In a large skillet, cook the garlic with the oil over medium heat, pressing the garlic once or twice with the back of a spoon. As soon as it is lightly browned, about 4 minutes, discard the garlic.

3. Add the peppers to the pan. Cook, stirring often, until softened, about 15 minutes.

4. Add the tomatoes and water. Cook until the sauce is thickened, about 15 minutes more.

5. Stir in the capers, anchovies, and almonds. Taste for salt. Cook 2 minutes more. Let cool slightly before serving.

Peppers with Tomatoes and Onions

Peperonata

Makes 4 servings

Every region seems to have its version of peperonata. Some add capers, olives, herbs, or anchovies. Serve this as a side dish or as a sauce for roast pork or grilled fish.

4 red or yellow bell peppers (or a mix)

2 medium onions, thinly sliced

3 tablespoons olive oil

3 large tomatoes, peeled, seeded, and coarsely chopped

1 garlic clove, finely chopped

Salt

1. Stand the peppers on a cutting board. Holding the stem in one hand, place the cutting edge of a large heavy chef's knife just beyond the edge of the cap. Cut straight down. Turn the pepper 90° and cut straight down again. Repeat, turning and cutting the remaining two sides. Discard the core, seeds, and stem, which will be in one piece. Cut away any membranes and scrape out any seeds. Cut the peppers into $1/4$-inch strips.

2. In a large skillet over medium heat, cook the onions in the olive oil until tender and golden, about 10 minutes. Add the pepper strips and cook 10 minutes more.

3. Stir in the tomatoes, garlic, and salt to taste. Cover and cook 20 minutes or until the peppers are tender when pierced with a knife. If there is a lot of liquid remaining, uncover and cook until the sauce is thickened and reduced. Serve hot or at room temperature.

Stuffed Frying Peppers

Peperoni Ripieni

Makes 4 to 8 servings

My grandmother always made these peppers in the summertime. She would cook them in a big black skillet in the morning, and by lunchtime they were just the right temperature for serving with sliced bread.

1¼ cups plain dry bread crumbs made from Italian or French bread

⅓ cup freshly grated Pecorino Romano or Parmigiano-Reggiano

¼ cup chopped fresh flat-leaf parsley

1 garlic clove, finely chopped

Salt and freshly ground black pepper

About ½ cup olive oil

8 long light-green Italian frying peppers

3 cups peeled, seeded, and chopped fresh tomatoes or 1 (28-ounce) can crushed tomatoes

6 fresh basil leaves, torn into bits

1. In a bowl, mix together the bread crumbs, cheese, parsley, garlic, and salt and pepper to taste. Stir in 3 tablespoons of the oil, or enough to moisten the crumbs evenly.

2. Cut off the tops of the peppers and scoop out the seeds. Spoon the bread crumb mixture into the peppers, leaving about 1 inch of clearance at the top. Do not overstuff the peppers, or the filling will spill out as the peppers cook.

3. In a large skillet, heat $1/4$ cup of oil over medium heat until a piece of pepper sizzles in the pan. With tongs, add the peppers carefully. Cook, turning occasionally with tongs, until browned on all sides, about 20 minutes.

4. Pour the tomatoes, basil, and salt and pepper to taste around the peppers. Bring to a simmer. Cover and cook, turning the peppers once or twice, until very tender, about 15 minutes. If the sauce is too dry, add a little water. Uncover and cook until the sauce is thick, about 5 minutes more. Serve warm or at room temperature.

Neapolitan-Style Stuffed Peppers

Peperoni alla Nonna

Makes 6 servings

If Sicilians have countless ways to cook eggplants, Neapolitans have the same creativity with peppers. This is another typical Neapolitan recipe that my grandmother used to make.

2 medium eggplants (about 1 pound each)

6 large red, yellow, or green bell peppers, cut into ½-inch strips

½ cup plus 3 tablespoons olive oil

3 medium tomatoes, peeled, seeded, and chopped

¾ cup pitted and chopped mild, oil-cured black olives, such as Gaeta

6 anchovy fillets, finely chopped

3 tablespoons capers, rinsed and drained

1 large garlic clove, peeled and finely chopped

3 tablespoons chopped fresh flat-leaf parsley

Freshly ground black pepper

½ cup plus 1 tablespoon plain bread crumbs

1. Trim the eggplants and cut them into ¾-inch cubes. Layer the pieces in a colander, sprinkling each layer with salt. Place the colander over a plate and let drain for 1 hour. Rinse the eggplant and pat dry with paper towels.

2. In a large skillet, heat the ½ cup of oil over medium heat. Add the eggplant and cook, stirring occasionally, until tender, about 10 minutes.

3. Stir in the tomatoes, olives, anchovies, capers, garlic, parsley, and pepper to taste. Bring to a simmer, then cook 5 minutes more. Stir in the ½ cup of bread crumbs and remove from the heat.

4. Place a rack in the center of the oven. Preheat the oven to 450°F. Oil a baking pan just large enough to hold the peppers upright.

5. Cut off the stems of the peppers and remove the seeds and white membranes. Stuff the eggplant mixture into the peppers. Stand the peppers in the prepared pan. Sprinkle with the remaining 1 tablespoon bread crumbs and drizzle with the remaining 3 tablespoons oil.

6. Pour 1 cup water around the peppers. Bake 1 hour 15 minutes or until the peppers are very tender and lightly browned. Serve hot or at room temperature.

Stuffed Peppers, Ada Boni's Style

Peperoni Ripieni alla Ada Boni

Makes 4 to 8 servings

Ada Boni was a famous Italian food writer and the author of numerous cookbooks. Her Italian Regional Cooking is a classic, and one of the first books on the subject translated into English. This recipe is adapted from the Sicily chapter.

4 medium red or yellow bell peppers

1 cup toasted plain bread crumbs

4 tablespoons raisins

½ cup chopped pitted mild black olives

6 anchovy fillets, chopped

2 tablespoons chopped fresh basil

2 tablespoons capers, rinsed, drained, and chopped

¼ cup plus 2 tablespoons olive oil

    1 cup Sicilian Tomato Sauce

1. Place a rack in the center of the oven. Preheat the oven to 375°F. Oil a 13 × 9 × 2–inch baking dish.

2. With a large heavy chef's knife, cut the peppers in half lengthwise. Cut out the stems, seeds, and white membranes.

3. In a large bowl, mix together the bread crumbs, raisins, olives, anchovies, basil, capers, and $1/4$ cup of the oil. Taste and adjust seasoning. (Salt will probably be unnecessary.)

4. Spoon the mixture into the pepper halves. Top with the sauce. Bake 50 minutes or until the peppers are very tender when pierced with a knife. Serve hot or at room temperature.

Fried Peppers

Peperoni Fritti

Makes 6 to 8 servings

Crisp and sweet, these are hard to resist. Serve them with an omelet or with any cooked meat.

4 large red or yellow bell peppers

½ cup all-purpose flour

Salt

1. Stand the peppers on a cutting board. Holding the stem in one hand, place the cutting edge of a large heavy chef's knife just beyond the edge of the cap. Cut straight down. Turn the pepper 90° and cut straight down again. Repeat, turning and cutting the remaining two sides. Discard the core, seeds, and stem, which will be in one piece. Cut away any membranes and scrape out any seeds. Cut the peppers into 1/4-inch strips.

2. Heat about 2 inches of oil in a deep heavy saucepan until the temperature reaches 375°F on a frying thermometer.

3. Line a tray with paper towels. Put the flour in a shallow bowl. Roll the pepper strips in the flour, shaking off the excess.

4. Add the peppers strips to the hot oil a few at a time. Fry until golden and tender, about 4 minutes. Drain on the paper towels. Fry the remainder in batches, in the same way. Sprinkle with salt and serve immediately.

Sautéed Peppers with Zucchini and Mint

Peperoni e Zucchini in Padella

Makes 6 servings

The longer this sits, the better it tastes, so make it early in the day to serve for a later meal.

1 red bell pepper

1 yellow bell pepper

2 tablespoons olive oil

4 small zucchini, cut into ¼-inch slices

Salt

2 tablespoons white wine vinegar

2 garlic cloves, very finely chopped

2 tablespoons chopped fresh mint

½ teaspoon dried oregano

Pinch of crushed red pepper

1. Stand the peppers on a cutting board. Holding the stem in one hand, place the cutting edge of a large heavy chef's knife just beyond the edge of the cap. Cut straight down. Turn the pepper 90° and cut straight down again. Repeat, turning and cutting the remaining two sides. Discard the core, seeds, and stem, which will be in one piece. Cut away any membranes and scrape out any seeds. Cut the peppers into 1-inch strips.

2. In a large skillet, heat the oil over medium heat. Add the peppers and cook, stirring, for 10 minutes.

3. Add the zucchini and salt to taste. Cook, stirring often, until the zucchini are tender, about 15 minutes.

4. While the vegetables are cooking, in a medium bowl, whisk together the vinegar, garlic, herbs, red pepper, and salt to taste.

5. Stir in the peppers and zucchini. Let stand until the vegetables are at room temperature. Taste and adjust seasoning.

Roasted Pepper and Eggplant Terrine

Sformato di Peperoni e Melanzane

Makes 8 to 12 servings

This is an unusual and beautiful terrine of layered peppers, eggplant, and flavorings. The pepper juices gel slightly after chilling and hold the terrine together. Serve it as a first course or as a side dish with grilled meats.

4 large red bell peppers, roasted and peeled

2 large eggplants (about 1½ pounds each)

Salt

Olive oil

½ cup torn fresh basil leaves

4 large garlic cloves, peeled, seeded, and finely chopped

¼ cup red wine vinegar

Freshly ground black pepper

1. Prepare the peppers, if necessary. Trim the eggplants and cut them lengthwise into $1/4$-inch-thick slices. Layer the slices in a colander, sprinkling each layer with salt. Let stand at least 30 minutes.

2. Preheat the oven to 450°F. Brush two large jelly roll pans with oil.

3. Rinse the eggplant slices in cool water and pat dry with paper towels. Arrange the eggplant in the pans in a single layer. Brush with oil. Bake the eggplant about 10 minutes, until lightly browned on top. Turn the pieces with tongs and bake about 10 minutes more or until tender and lightly browned.

4. Drain the peppers and cut them into 1-inch strips.

5. Line an 8 × 4 × 3–inch loaf pan with plastic wrap. Place a layer of eggplant slices in the bottom of the pan, overlapping them slightly. Make a layer of the roasted peppers over the eggplant. Sprinkle with some of the basil, garlic, vinegar, oil, and salt and pepper to taste. Continue layering, pressing each layer down firmly, until all of the ingredients are used. Cover with plastic wrap and weight the contents with a second loaf pan filled with heavy cans. Refrigerate for at least 24 hours or up to 3 days.

6. To serve, uncover the terrine and invert it onto a serving place. Carefully remove the plastic wrap. Cut the terrine into thick slices. Serve cold or at room temperature.

Sweet-and-Sour Potatoes

Patate in Agrodolce

Makes 6 to 8 servings

This is a Sicilian-style potato salad to serve at room temperature with grilled pork ribs, chicken, or sausages.

2 pounds all-purpose potatoes, such as Yukon gold

1 onion

2 tablespoons olive oil

1 cup pitted mild black olives, such as Gaeta

2 tablespoons capers

Salt and freshly ground black pepper

2 tablespoons white wine vinegar

2 tablespoons sugar

1. Scrub the potatoes with a brush under cold running water. Peel them if desired. Cut the potatoes into halves or quarters if large.

In a large skillet, cook the onion in the oil until tender and golden, about 10 minutes.

2. Stir in the potatoes, olives, capers, and salt and pepper to taste. Add 1 cup of water and bring to a simmer. Cook 15 minutes.

3. In a small bowl, stir together the vinegar and sugar, and add it to the skillet. Continue to cook until the potatoes are tender, about 5 minutes. Remove from the heat and let cool completely. Serve at room temperature.

Potatoes with Balsamic Vinegar

Patate al Balsamico

Makes 6 servings

Red onion and balsamic vinegar flavor these potatoes. They are good at room temperature, too.

2 pounds all-purpose potatoes, such as Yukon gold

2 tablespoons olive oil

1 large red onion, chopped

2 tablespoons water

Salt and freshly ground black pepper

2 tablespoons balsamic vinegar

1. Scrub the potatoes with a brush under cold running water. Peel them if desired. Cut the potatoes into halves or quarters if large.

2. Heat the oil in a medium saucepan over medium heat. Add the potatoes, onion, water, and salt and pepper to taste. Cover the pan and reduce the heat to low. Cook 20 minutes or until the potatoes are tender.

3. Uncover the pan and stir in the vinegar. Cook until most of the liquid evaporates, about 5 minutes. Serve hot or at room temperature.

Venetian-Style Potatoes

Patate alla Veneziana

Makes 4 servings

Though I use Yukon gold potatoes for most cooking, there are many other good varieties available, especially at farmer's markets, and they add variety to potato dishes. Yellow Finn potatoes are good for roasting and baking, and Red Russians are excellent in salads. Though odd looking, blue potatoes can be very good too.

1¼ pounds all-purpose potatoes, such as Yukon gold

2 tablespoons unsalted butter

1 tablespoon olive oil

1 medium onion, chopped

Salt and freshly ground black pepper

2 tablespoons chopped fresh flat-leaf parsley

1. Scrub the potatoes with a brush under cold running water. Peel them if desired. Cut the potatoes into halves or quarters if large. In a large skillet, melt the butter with the oil over medium heat. Add the onion and cook until softened, about 5 minutes.

2. Add the potatoes and salt and pepper to taste. Cover the pan and cook, stirring occasionally, about 20 minutes, or until the potatoes are tender.

3. Add the parsley and stir well. Serve hot.

"Jumped" Potatoes

Patate al Salto

Makes 4 servings

When you order fried potatoes in an Italian restaurant, this is what you get. The potatoes become lightly crusty on the outside and soft and creamy inside. They are called "jumped" potatoes because they need frequent stirring or tossing in the pan.

1¼ pounds all-purpose potatoes, such as Yukon gold

¼ cup olive oil

Salt and freshly ground black pepper

1. Scrub the potatoes with a brush under cold running water. Peel the potatoes. Cut them into 1-inch pieces.

2. Pour the oil into a 9-inch skillet. Place the pan over medium-high heat until the oil is very hot and a piece of potato sizzles when added.

3. Dry the potatoes well with paper towels. Add the potatoes to the hot oil and let cook 2 minutes. Turn the potatoes and cook 2 minutes more. Continue cooking and turning the potatoes every

2 minutes or until lightly browned on all sides, about 10 minutes in all.

4. Add salt and pepper to taste. Cover the pan and cook, turning occasionally, until the potatoes are tender when pierced with a knife, about 5 minutes. Serve immediately.

Variation: *Potatoes with Garlic and Herbs*: In step 4 add 2 garlic cloves, chopped, and a tablespoon of chopped fresh rosemary or sage.

Potato-Pepper Sauté

Patate e Peperoni in Padella

Makes 6 servings

Peppers, garlic, and hot red pepper flavor this tasty sauté.

1¼ pounds all-purpose potatoes, such as Yukon gold

4 tablespoons olive oil

2 large red or yellow bell peppers, cut into 1-inch pieces

Salt

¼ cup chopped fresh flat-leaf parsley

2 large garlic cloves

Pinch of crushed red pepper

1. Scrub the potatoes with a brush under cold running water. Peel the potatoes and cut them into 1-inch pieces.

2. In a large skillet, heat 2 tablespoons of the oil over medium heat. Dry the potatoes well with paper towels and place them in the pan. Cook, stirring the potatoes from time to time, until they

begin to turn brown, about 10 minutes. Sprinkle with salt. Cover the pan and cook 10 minutes.

3. While the potatoes cook, in another skillet, heat the remaining 2 tablespoons oil over medium heat. Add the bell peppers and salt to taste. Cook, stirring occasionally, until the peppers are almost tender, about 10 minutes.

4. Stir the potatoes, then add the peppers. Stir in the parsley, garlic, and crushed red pepper. Cook until the potatoes are tender, about 5 minutes. Serve hot.

Mashed Potatoes with Parsley and Garlic

Patate Schiacciate all'Aglio e Prezzemolo

Makes 4 servings

Mashed potatoes get an Italian treatment with parsley, garlic, and olive oil. If you like your potatoes spicy, stir in a big pinch of crushed red pepper.

1¼ pounds all-purpose potatoes, such as Yukon gold

Salt

¼ cup olive oil

1 large garlic clove, finely chopped

1 tablespoon chopped fresh flat-leaf parsley

Freshly ground black pepper

1. Scrub the potatoes with a brush under cold running water. Peel the potatoes and cut them into quarters. Place the potatoes in a medium saucepan with cold water to cover and salt to taste. Cover and bring to a simmer. Cook 15 minutes or until the potatoes are tender when pierced with a knife. Drain the potatoes, reserving some of the water.

2. Dry the pan in which the potatoes were cooked. Add 2 tablespoons of the oil and the garlic and cook over medium heat until the garlic is just fragrant, about 1 minute. Add the potatoes and parsley to the pan. Mash the potatoes with a masher or a fork, stirring them well to blend them with the garlic and parsley. Add the remaining oil, and salt and pepper to taste. Add a little of the cooking water if needed. Serve immediately.

Variation: *Mashed Potatoes with Olives*: Stir in 2 tablespoons chopped black or green olives just before serving.

Herbed New Potatoes with Pancetta

Patatine alle Erbe Aromatiche

Makes 4 servings

Little new potatoes are delicious cooked this way. (New potatoes are not a variety. Any freshly dug potato with thin skin can be called a new potato.) Use an all-purpose potato if new potatoes are not available.

1¼ pounds small new potatoes

2 ounces sliced pancetta, diced

1 medium onion, chopped

2 tablespoons olive oil

1 garlic clove, finely chopped

6 fresh basil leaves, torn into bits

1 teaspoon chopped fresh rosemary

1 bay leaf

Salt and freshly ground black pepper

1. Scrub the potatoes with a brush under cold running water. Peel them if desired. Cut the potatoes into 1-inch pieces.

2. Combine the pancetta, onion, and olive oil in a large skillet. Cook over medium heat until softened, about 5 minutes.

3. Add the potatoes and cook, stirring occasionally, for 10 minutes.

4. Stir in the garlic, basil, rosemary, bay leaf, and salt and pepper to taste. Cover the pan and cook for 20 minutes more, stirring occasionally, until the potatoes are tender when pierced with a fork. Add a little water if the potatoes begin to brown too rapidly.

5. Remove the bay leaf and serve hot.

Potatoes with Tomatoes and Onions

Patate alla Pizzaiola

Makes 6 to 8 servings.

Potatoes roasted with pizza flavors are typical in Naples and elsewhere in the south.

2 pounds all-purpose potatoes, such as Yukon gold

2 large tomatoes, peeled, seeded, and chopped

2 medium onions, sliced

1 garlic clove, finely chopped

½ teaspoon dried oregano

¼ cup olive oil

Salt and freshly ground black pepper

1. Preheat the oven to 450°F. Scrub the potatoes with a brush under cold running water. Peel them if desired. Cut the potatoes into 1-inch pieces. In a baking pan large enough to hold the ingredients in a single layer, toss together the potatoes, tomatoes, onions, garlic, oregano, oil, and salt and pepper to taste. Spread the ingredients out evenly in the pan.

2. Place a rack in the center of the oven. Roast the vegetables, stirring 2 or 3 times, for 1 hour or until the potatoes are cooked through. Serve hot.

Roasted Potatoes with Garlic and Rosemary

Patate Arrosto

Makes 4 servings

I can never make enough of these crusty brown potatoes. No one can resist them. The trick to making them is to use a pan large enough so that the potato pieces are barely touching and not piled on top of one another. If your roasting pan is not large enough, use a 15 × 10 × 1–inch jelly roll pan, or use two smaller pans.

2 pounds all-purpose potatoes, such as Yukon gold

¼ cup olive oil

1 tablespoon chopped fresh rosemary

Salt and freshly ground black pepper

2 garlic cloves, finely chopped

1. Place a rack in the center of the oven. Preheat the oven to 400°F. Scrub the potatoes with a brush under cold running water. Peel them if desired. Cut the potatoes into 1-inch pieces. Dry the potatoes with paper towels. Put them in a roasting pan large enough to hold the potatoes in a single layer. Drizzle with the oil and toss with the rosemary and salt and pepper to taste. Spread the potatoes out evenly.

2. Roast the potatoes, stirring every 15 minutes, for 45 minutes. Stir in the garlic and cook 15 minutes more or until the potatoes are tender. Serve hot.

Roasted Potatoes with Mushrooms

Patate e Funghi al Forno

Makes 6 servings

The potatoes pick up some of the mushroom and garlic aromas as they roast in the same pan.

1½ pounds all-purpose potatoes, such as Yukon gold

1 pound mushrooms, any kind, halved or quartered if large

¼ cup olive oil

2 to 3 garlic cloves, thinly sliced

Salt and freshly ground black pepper

2 tablespoons chopped fresh flat-leaf parsley

1. Place a rack in the center of the oven. Preheat the oven to 400°F. Scrub the potatoes with a brush under cold running water. Peel them if desired. Cut the potatoes into 1-inch pieces. Place the potatoes and mushrooms in a large roasting pan. Toss the vegetables with the oil, garlic, and a generous sprinkle of salt and pepper.

2. Roast the vegetables 15 minutes. Toss them well. Bake 30 minutes more, stirring occasionally, or until the potatoes are tender. Sprinkle with chopped parsley and serve hot.

Potatoes and Cauliflower, Basilicata Style

Patate e Cavolfiore al Forno

Makes 4 to 6

Put a pan of potatoes and cauliflower in the oven alongside a roast pork or chicken for a fine Sunday dinner. The vegetables should be crisp and brown around the edges, their flavors enhanced by the perfume of the oregano.

1 small cauliflower

¼ cup olive oil

3 medium all-purpose potatoes, such as Yukon gold quartered

½ teaspoon dried oregano, crumbled

Salt and freshly ground black pepper

1. Cut the cauliflower into 2-inch florets. Trim off the ends of the stems. Cut thick stems crosswise into 1/4-inch slices.

2. Place a rack in the center of the oven. Preheat the oven to 400°F. Pour the oil into a 13 × 9 × 2– inch roasting pan. Add the

vegetables and toss well. Sprinkle with the oregano and salt and pepper to taste. Toss again.

3. Bake 45 minutes or until the vegetables are tender and browned. Serve hot.

Potatoes and Cabbage in the Pan

Patate e Cavolo in Tegame

Makes 4 to 6 servings

Versions of this dish exist all over Italy. In Friuli, smoked pancetta is added to the skillet with the onion. I like this simple version from Basilicata. The pale pink of the onion complements the creamy white potatoes and green cabbage. The potatoes become so soft that they are like mashed potatoes by the time the cabbage is tender.

3 tablespoons olive oil

1 medium red onion, chopped

½ head medium cabbage, thinly sliced (about 4 cups)

3 medium all-purpose potatoes, such as Yukon gold, peeled and cut into bite-size pieces

½ cup water

Salt and freshly ground black pepper

1. Pour the oil into a large skillet. Add the onion and cook over medium heat, stirring frequently, until softened, about 5 minutes.

2. Stir in the cabbage, potatoes, water, and salt and pepper to taste. Cover and cook, stirring occasionally, 30 minutes or until the vegetables are soft. Add a little more water if the vegetables begin to stick. Serve hot.

Potato and Spinach Torte

Torta di Patate e Spinaci

Makes 8 servings

When I had this layered vegetable torte in Rome, it was made with chicory instead of spinach. Roman chicory looks something like young dandelion or mature arugula. Spinach is a good stand-in for the chicory. For best flavor, be sure to let this dish cool slightly before serving it.

2 pounds all-purpose potatoes, such as Yukon gold

Salt

4 tablespoons unsalted butter

1 small onion, very finely chopped

1½ pounds spinach, chicory, dandelion, or Swiss chard, trimmed

½ cup water

½ cup hot milk

1 cup freshly grated Parmigiano-Reggiano

Freshly ground black pepper

1 tablespoon plain bread crumbs

1. Scrub the potatoes with a brush under cold running water. Peel the potatoes and place them in a medium pot with cold water to cover. Add salt and cover the pot. Bring to a boil and cook about 20 minutes, or until the potatoes are tender.

2. In a small skillet, melt 2 tablespoons of the butter over medium heat. Add the onion and cook, stirring often, until the onion is tender and golden.

3. Place the spinach in a large pot with the $1/2$ cup of water and salt to taste. Cover and cook until tender, about 5 minutes. Drain well and squeeze out the excess liquid. Chop the spinach on a board.

4. Add the spinach to the skillet and stir it together with the onion.

5. When the potatoes are tender, drain them and mash them until smooth. Stir in the remaining 2 tablespoons of butter and the milk. Add $3/4$ cup of the cheese and mix well. Season to taste with salt and pepper.

6. Place a rack in the center of the oven. Preheat the oven to 375°F.

7. Generously butter a 9-inch baking dish. Spread half the potatoes in the dish. Make a second layer of all of the spinach. Top with the remaining potatoes. Sprinkle with the remaining $1/4$ cup of cheese and the bread crumbs.

8. Bake 45 to 50 minutes or until the top is golden. Let rest 15 minutes before serving.

Neapolitan Potato Croquettes

Panzerotti or Crocche

Makes about 24

In Naples, pizzerias set up sidewalk stands to sell these tasty logs of mashed potatoes in a crisp bread-crumb jacket, making them easy for passersby to eat for lunch or a snack. This, however, is my grandmother's recipe. We ate potato croquettes for holidays and festive occasions all year round, usually as a side dish with roast beef.

2½ pounds all-purpose potatoes, such as Yukon gold

3 large eggs

1 cup freshly grated Pecorino Romano or Parmigiano-Reggiano

2 tablespoons chopped fresh flat-leaf parsley

¼ cup finely chopped salame (about 2 ounces)

Salt and freshly ground black pepper

2 cups plain dry bread crumbs

Vegetable oil for frying

1. Scrub the potatoes with a brush under cold running water. Place the potatoes in a large saucepan with cold water to cover. Cover the pan and bring the water to a boil. Cook over medium heat until the potatoes are tender when pierced with a fork, about 20 minutes. Drain the potatoes, then let them cool slightly. Peel the potatoes. Put them in a large bowl and mash them with a masher or fork until smooth.

2. Separate the eggs, putting the yolks in a small bowl and setting the whites aside in a shallow dish. Spread the bread crumbs on a sheet of wax paper.

3. Stir the egg yolks, cheese, parsley, and salame into the mashed potatoes. Add salt and pepper to taste.

4. Using about $1/4$ cup of the potato mixture, form a sausage shape about 1 inch wide and $2 1/2$ inches long. Repeat with the remaining potatoes.

5. Beat the egg whites with a whisk or a fork until frothy. Dip the potato logs into the whites, then roll them in the crumbs, coating them completely. Place the logs on a wire rack and let dry 15 to 30 minutes.

6. Pour about $1/2$ inch of the oil into a large heavy skillet. Heat over medium heat until a bit of the egg white sizzles when dropped in

the oil. Carefully place some of the logs in the pan, leaving a little space between them. Fry them, turning occasionally with tongs, until evenly browned, about 10 minutes. Transfer the browned croquettes to paper towels to drain.

7. Serve immediately or keep the croquettes warm in a low oven while frying the remainder.

Dad's Neapolitan Potato Pie

Gatto'

Makes 6 to 8 servings

Gatto' comes from the French gateau, meaning "cake." The derivation leads me to think this recipe was made popular by the French-trained monzu—chefs who cooked for the aristocrats at the court of Naples.

In our house, we called this potato pie, and if we weren't having potato croquettes with our Sunday dinner, we had this potato dish, which was my father's specialty.

2½ pounds all-purpose potatoes, such as Yukon gold

Salt

¼ cup plain dry bread crumbs

4 tablespoons (½ stick) unsalted butter, softened

1 cup warm milk

1 cup plus 2 tablespoons freshly grated Parmigiano-Reggiano

1 large egg, beaten

¼ teaspoon freshly grated nutmeg

Salt and freshly ground black pepper

8 ounces fresh mozzarella, chopped

4 ounces salame or imported Italian prosciutto, chopped

1. Scrub the potatoes with a brush under cold running water. Place the potatoes in a large saucepan with cold water to cover. Add salt to taste. Cover the pan and bring the water to a boil. Cook over medium heat until the potatoes are tender when pierced with a fork, about 20 minutes. Drain and let cool slightly.

2. Place a rack in the center of the oven. Preheat the oven to 400°F. Butter a 2-quart baking dish. Sprinkle with the bread crumbs.

3. Peel the potatoes, put them in a large bowl, and mash them with a masher or fork until smooth. Stir in 3 tablespoons of the butter, the milk, 1 cup of the Parmigiano, the egg, nutmeg, and salt and pepper to taste. Fold in the mozzarella and salame.

4. Spread the mixture evenly in the prepared dish. Sprinkle with the remaining Parmigiano. Dot with the remaining 1 tablespoon butter.

5. Bake 35 to 45 minutes or until the top is browned. Let stand briefly at room temperature before serving.

Skillet Tomatoes

Pomodori in Padella

Makes 6 to 8 servings

Serve these as a side dish with grilled or roasted meats, or at room temperature, mashed onto toasted country bread as an appetizer.

8 plum tomatoes

¼ cup olive oil

2 garlic cloves, finely chopped

2 tablespoons chopped fresh basil

Salt and freshly ground black pepper

1. Rinse the tomatoes and pat dry. With a small knife, cut around the stem end of each tomato and remove it. Cut the tomatoes in half lengthwise.

2. In a large skillet, heat the oil with the garlic and basil over medium heat. Add the tomato halves cut-side down. Sprinkle with salt and pepper. Cook until the tomatoes are browned and tender, about 10 minutes. Serve hot or at room temperature.

Steamed Tomatoes

Pomodori al Vapore

Makes 4 servings

Here, sweet little tomatoes are cooked in their own juices. Serve them as a side dish with meat or fish, or spoon them over a frittata. If the tomatoes are not quite sweet enough, add a pinch of sugar as they cook.

1 pint cherry or grape tomatoes

2 tablespoons extra-virgin olive oil

Salt

6 basil leaves, stacked and cut into narrow strips

1. Rinse the tomatoes and pat dry. Cut them in half through the stem end. In a small saucepan, combine the tomatoes, oil, and salt. Cover the pan and place on low heat. Cook 10 minutes or until the tomatoes are just softened but still hold their shape.

2. Add the basil. Serve hot or at room temperature.

Baked Tomatoes

Pomodori al Forno

Makes 8 servings

A bread-crumb topping seasons these tomatoes. They are good with roasted fish and most egg dishes.

8 plum tomatoes

1 cup bread crumbs

4 anchovy fillets, finely chopped

2 tablespoons capers, rinsed and drained

½ cup freshly grated Pecorino Romano

½ teaspoon dried oregano

3 tablespoons olive oil

Salt and freshly ground black pepper

1. Rinse and dry the tomatoes. Cut the tomatoes in half lengthwise. With a small spoon, scoop out the seeds into a fine-mesh strainer set over a bowl to collect the juices. In a large skillet, toast the bread crumbs over medium heat, stirring often, until they are just fragrant, not browned, about 5 minutes. Remove from the heat and let cool slightly.

2. Place a rack in the center of the oven. Preheat the oven to 400°F. Oil a large baking pan. Arrange the tomato shells cut-side up in the pan.

3. To the bowl with the tomato juice, add the bread crumbs, anchovies, capers, cheese, oregano, and salt and pepper. Stir in 2 tablespoons of the olive oil. Stuff the mixture into the tomato shells. Drizzle with the remaining tablespoon of oil.

4. Bake 40 minutes or until the tomatoes are tender and the crumbs are golden. Serve hot.

Tomatoes Stuffed with Farro

Pomodori Ripieni

Makes 4 servings

Farro, an ancient grain that is popular in Italy, makes a great stuffing for tomatoes when mixed with cheese and onion. I had something like this at L'Angolo Divino, a wine bar in Rome.

1 cup semipearled farro (or substitute wheat berries or bulgur)

Salt

4 large round tomatoes

1 small onion, finely chopped

2 tablespoons olive oil

¼ cup grated Pecorino Romano or Parmigiano-Reggiano

Freshly ground black pepper

1. In a medium saucepan, bring 4 cups of water to a boil. Add the farro and salt to taste. Cook until the farro is tender but still chewy, about 30 minutes. Drain the farro and place it in a bowl.

2. In a small saucepan, cook the onion in the oil over medium heat until golden, about 10 minutes.

3. Place a rack in the center of the oven. Preheat the oven to 350°F. Oil a small baking pan just large enough to hold the tomatoes.

4. Rinse and dry the tomatoes. Cut a slice $1/2$ inch thick from the top of each tomato and reserve. With a small spoon, scoop out the insides of the tomatoes and place the pulp in a fine-mesh strainer set over a bowl. Arrange the tomato shells in the baking dish.

5. To the bowl with the farro, add the strained tomato liquid, sautéed onion, cheese, and salt and pepper to taste. Spoon the mixture into the tomato shells. Cover the tomatoes with the reserved tops.

6. Bake 20 minutes or until the tomatoes are tender. Serve hot or at room temperature.

Roman Stuffed Tomatoes

Pomodori Ripieni alla Romana

Makes 6 servings

This is a classic Roman dish, typically eaten at room temperature as a first course.

¾ cup medium-grain rice, such as Arborio, Carnaroli, or Vialone Nano

Salt

6 large round tomatoes

4 tablespoons olive oil

3 anchovy fillets, finely chopped

1 small garlic clove, finely chopped

¼ cup chopped fresh basil

¼ cup freshly grated Parmigiano-Reggiano

1. Bring 1 quart of water to a boil over high heat. Add the rice and 1 teaspoon salt. Reduce the heat to low and simmer for 10

minutes or until the rice is partially cooked but still very firm. Drain well. Put the rice in a large bowl.

2. Place a rack in the center of the oven. Preheat the oven to 350°F. Oil a baking pan just large enough to hold the tomatoes.

3. Cut a 1/2-inch slice from the top of the tomatoes and reserve. With a small spoon, scoop out the insides of the tomatoes and place the pulp in a fine-mesh strainer set over a bowl. Place the tomato shells in the pan.

4. To the bowl with the rice, add the strained tomato liquid and the oil, anchovies, garlic, basil, cheese, and salt to taste. Stir well. Spoon the mixture into the tomato shells. Cover the tomatoes with the reserved tops.

5. Bake 20 minutes or until the rice is tender. Serve hot or at room temperature.

Roasted Tomatoes with Balsamic Vinegar

Pomodori al Balsamico

Makes 6 servings

Balsamic vinegar has a nearly magical way of enhancing the flavor of vegetables. Try this simple dish and serve it as an appetizer or with meats.

8 plum tomatoes

2 tablespoons olive oil

1 tablespoon balsamic vinegar

Salt and freshly ground black pepper

1. Place a rack in the center of the oven. Preheat the oven to 375°F. Oil a baking dish large enough to hold the tomatoes in a single layer.

2. Rinse the tomatoes and pat dry. Cut the tomatoes in half lengthwise. Scoop out the tomato seeds. Place the tomato halves cut-sides up in the pan. Drizzle with the oil and vinegar and sprinkle with salt and pepper.

3. Bake the tomatoes 45 minutes or until tender. Serve at room temperature.

ZUCCHINI AND WINTER SQUASH

Practically every part of the zucchini plant is edible. Sicilians make soup out of the green leaves and vines, known as *tenerumi*. Zucchini and other large squash flowers are stuffed with meat or cheese and fried or poached. The zucchini themselves are used in countless preparations.

Occasionally, I find pale green *romanesco* zucchini in my farmer's market. These are more flavorful than the familiar dark green variety and less watery. The most important thing about zucchini is to choose the smallest ones you can find. They have fewer and more tender seeds and more flavor. The gigantic zucchini generous gardeners are always trying to foist on unsuspecting friends are watery and all but useless.

Winter squashes are sold by the slice in Italy. The varieties used there are often very large, but their texture is similar to the hard squashes found in the United States. Most of the time I rely on butternut squash, which are sweet and buttery, though acorn, Hubbard, or pumpkin can also be used.

Zucchini Carpaccio

Carpaccio in Giallo e Verde

Makes 4 servings

I first ate a simpler version of this refreshing salad at the home of winemaker friends in Tuscany. Over the years, I have embellished it by using a combination of yellow and green zucchini and adding fresh mint.

2 or 3 small zucchini, preferably a mix of yellow and green

3 tablespoons fresh lemon juice

⅓ cup extra-virgin olive oil

Salt and freshly ground black pepper

2 tablespoons finely chopped fresh mint

About 2 ounces Parmigiano-Reggiano, in 1 piece

1. Scrub the zucchini with a brush under cold running water. Trim off the ends.

2. In a food processor or on a mandoline slicer, cut the zucchini into very thin slices. Place the slices in a medium bowl.

3. In a small bowl, whisk together the lemon juice, olive oil, and salt and pepper to taste until blended. Stir in the mint. Drizzle over the zucchini and toss well. Spread the slices out on a shallow platter.

4. With a vegetable peeler, shave the Parmigiano into thin slices. Scatter the slices over the zucchini. Serve immediately.

Zucchini with Garlic and Mint

Zucchine a Scapece

Makes 8 servings

Zucchini or other squash, eggplant, and carrots can be prepared a scapece, "in the style of Apicius," an early Roman who wrote about food. The vegetables are fried, flavored, and then chilled. Be sure to make this at least 24 hours before serving for best flavor.

2 pounds small zucchini

Vegetable oil for frying

3 tablespoons red wine vinegar

2 large garlic cloves, finely chopped

1/4 cup chopped fresh mint or basil

Salt and freshly ground black pepper

1. Scrub the zucchini with a brush under cold running water. Trim off the ends. Cut the zucchini into 1/4-inch slices.

2. Pour 1 inch of oil into a deep heavy skillet or wide saucepan. Heat the oil over medium heat until a small piece of vegetable dropped into the oil sizzles.

3. Pat the zucchini slices dry with paper towels. Carefully slip about one-fourth of the zucchini into the hot oil. Cook until lightly browned around the edges, about 3 minutes. With a slotted spoon, transfer the zucchini to paper towels to drain. Fry the remainder in the same way.

4. Layer the zucchini in a dish, sprinkling each layer with some of the vinegar, garlic, mint, and salt and pepper to taste. Cover and refrigerate at least 24 hours before serving.

Sautéed Zucchini

Zucchine in Padella

Makes 6 servings

This is a quick way to make a tasty side dish with zucchini, onions, and parsley.

1 pound small zucchini

2 tablespoons unsalted butter

1 small onion, very finely chopped

Salt and freshly ground black pepper

3 tablespoons chopped flat-leaf parsley

1. Scrub the zucchini with a brush under cold running water. Trim off the ends. Cut into $1/8$-inch slices.

2. In a medium skillet over medium-low heat, melt the butter. Add the onion and cook until softened, about 5 minutes.

3. Add the zucchini and toss to coat with the butter. Cover and cook 5 minutes, or until the zucchini is just tender when pierced with a fork.

4. Add the salt and pepper to taste and parsley and toss well. Serve immediately.

Zucchini with Prosciutto

Zucchine al Prosciutto

Makes 4 servings

These zucchini are good as a side dish with chicken, but also as a sauce for hot cooked penne or another pasta.

1½ pounds small zucchini

1 medium onion, chopped

2 tablespoons olive oil

1 garlic clove, chopped

½ teaspoon dried marjoram or thyme

Salt and freshly ground black pepper

3 thin slices imported Italian prosciutto, cut crosswise into narrow strips

1. Scrub the zucchini with a brush under cold running water. Trim off the ends. Cut the zucchini into $1/8$-inch slices.

2. In a large skillet, cook the onion in the oil over medium heat. Cook, stirring, until the onion is tender and golden, about 10 minutes. Add the garlic and marjoram and cook 1 minute more.

3. Stir in the zucchini slices and salt and pepper to taste. Cook 5 minutes.

4. Add the prosciutto and cook until the zucchini are tender, about 2 minutes more. Serve hot.

Zucchini with Parmesan Crumbs

Zucchine alla Parmigiana

Makes 4 servings

Buttery, cheesy bread crumbs flavor this zucchini gratin.

1 pound small zucchini

2 tablespoons unsalted butter, melted and cooled

2 tablespoons bread crumbs, preferably homemade

¼ cup grated Parmigiano-Reggiano

Salt and freshly ground pepper

1. Scrub the zucchini with a brush under cold running water. Trim off the ends.

2. Place a rack in the center of the oven. Preheat oven to 425°F. Butter a 13 × 9 × 2–inch baking dish.

3. Spread the zucchini slices in the baking dish, overlapping slightly. In a medium bowl, mix together the butter, crumbs, cheese, and salt and pepper to taste. Sprinkle the crumb mixture over the zucchini.

4. Bake 30 minutes or until the crumbs are golden and the zucchini are tender. Serve hot.

Zucchini Gratin

Zucchine Gratinate

Makes 4 to 6 servings

When I think of this gratin, I imagine serving it as part of a summer picnic buffet, with grilled meat or fish and several salads. It is good hot or cold.

2 medium yellow onions, chopped

2 garlic cloves, finely chopped

4 tablespoons olive oil

Salt and freshly ground black pepper

1 tablespoon chopped fresh thyme, basil, or oregano

4 small zucchini, cut into $1/8$-inch slices

3 medium round tomatoes, cut into thin slices

$1/2$ cup grated Parmigiano-Reggiano

1. In a medium skillet, cook the onions and garlic in 2 tablespoons of the olive oil over medium-low heat until golden, about 10 minutes. Season with salt and pepper to taste.

2. Place a rack in the center of the oven. Preheat the oven to 375°F. Oil a 13 × 9 × 2–inch baking dish.

3. Spread the onion mixture evenly in the baking dish. Scatter one-third of the thyme over the onions. Arrange the zucchini and tomatoes in overlapping slices over the onions. Sprinkle with the remaining thyme, and salt and pepper to taste. Drizzle with the remaining olive oil.

4. Bake 40 to 45 minutes or until the vegetables are tender and the juices are sizzling. Sprinkle with the cheese and bake until slightly melted, about 5 minutes more. Let rest 10 minutes before serving.

Zucchini with Tomatoes and Anchovies

Zucchine al Forno

Makes 4 servings

This southern-style gratin is flavored with anchovies and garlic.

1 pound small zucchini

4 plum tomatoes, thinly sliced

¼ cup plain dry bread crumbs

3 anchovy fillets, chopped

2 tablespoons olive oil

1 small garlic clove, finely chopped

Salt and freshly ground black pepper

1. Scrub the zucchini with a brush under cold running water. Trim off the ends. Cut into $1/8$-inch slices.

2. Place a rack in the center of the oven. Preheat the oven to 375°F. Oil a 13 × 9 × 2–inch baking pan. Arrange the zucchini and tomatoes in overlapping rows in the pan.

3. In a medium bowl, stir together the bread crumbs, anchovies, oil, garlic, and salt and pepper to taste. Scatter the mixture over the vegetables.

4. Bake 30 minutes, or until the vegetables are tender. Let rest 10 minutes before serving.

Zucchini Stew

Ciambotta di Zucchine

Makes 4 to 6 servings

Here is another member of the southern Italian ciambotta family of vegetable stews, one that my mom used to make again and again in the summer when I was growing up. Though I wasn't fond of it as a child, because we had it so often, I enjoy it—once in a while—now.

3 small to medium zucchini

2 medium onions, chopped

3 tablespoons olive oil

1 garlic clove, very finely chopped

4 plum tomatoes, cut into bite-size pieces

2 medium potatoes, peeled and cut into bite-size pieces

Salt and freshly ground black pepper

2 tablespoons chopped fresh basil

1. Scrub the zucchini with a brush under cold running water. Trim off the ends. Cut the zucchini into bite-size pieces.

2. In a large saucepan, cook the onions in the oil over medium heat until softened, about 5 minutes. Stir in the garlic and cook 1 minute more.

3. Add the tomatoes, zucchini, potatoes, and salt and pepper to taste. Cover and cook, stirring occasionally, 30 minutes or until the potatoes are very tender. Add a little water if the mixture seems dry.

4. When the ciambotta is done, remove from the heat and stir in the basil. Serve hot or at room temperature.

Abruzzo-Style Almond Cake with Chocolate Frosting

Parozzo

Makes 8 servings

Parozzo is an Abbruzzese dialect word meaning "rough bread," though nowadays it also indicates this lovely almond cake. I have sampled versions baked in everything from long loaf shapes to small cupcake pans.

1 cup all-purpose flour

1 teaspoon baking powder

½ teaspoon salt

1 cup blanched almonds

1 cup sugar

½ cup plus 2 tablespoons unsalted butter

3 large eggs

1 teaspoon pure vanilla extract

¼ teaspoon almond extract

4 ounces bittersweet or semisweet chocolate, chopped

1 tablespoon slivered almonds, toasted and cooled

1. Place the rack in the center of the oven. Preheat the oven to 375°F. Grease and flour a 9 × 2-inch round cake pan. Tap out the excess flour.

2. In a large bowl, sift together the flour, baking powder, and salt.

3. In a food processor, grind the almonds with ¼ cup of the sugar until very fine.

4. In a large bowl, with an electric mixer at medium speed, beat ½ cup of the butter with the remaining ¾ cup of sugar until light and fluffy. Beat in the eggs and extracts until blended. Add the ground almond mixture and stir until smooth.

5. Scrape the batter into the prepared pan. Bake 30 minutes or until the cake is golden brown and a toothpick inserted in the center comes out clean.

6. Cool the cake in the pan on a wire rack 10 minutes. Invert the cake onto the rack. Turn it right side up onto another rack and let cool completely.

7. Bring about 2 inches of water to a simmer in the bottom half of a double boiler or a small saucepan. Place the chocolate and the remaining 2 tablespoons of butter in the top half of the double boiler or in a small heatproof bowl that fits comfortably over the saucepan. Place the bowl over the simmering water. Let stand uncovered until the chocolate is softened. Stir until smooth.

8. Pour half the chocolate over the cake, allowing some to drip over the sides. Smooth the sides and top. Spread the remaining glaze over the cake swirling it with a spatula. Sprinkle with the slivered almonds. Let set at room temperature at least 30 minutes before serving. Cover with a large inverted bowl and store in the refrigerator up to 3 days.

Rum and Currant Loaf Cakes

Plumcake

Makes two 8 × 4–inch loaf cakes

Currants and rum are the main flavoring in this Italian-style tea cake, known as plumcake, even though it contains no plums. The cake is probably an adaptation of an English recipe and has retained its English name.

The combination of cake flour and potato starch makes it feather light. The recipe makes two loaves, so you can freeze one or give it away.

1 cup currants or dark raisins

1 cup plain cake flour

½ cup potato starch or cornstarch

1 teaspoon baking powder

½ pound (2 sticks) unsalted butter, at room temperature

1 cup sugar

4 large eggs, at room temperature

⅓ cup dark rum or brandy

1. Place a rack in the center of the oven. Preheat the oven to 325°F. Butter and flour two 8 × 4– inch loaf pans. Tap out the excess flour.

2. Toss the currants with 2 tablespoons of the flour. Set aside.

3. Place the remaining flour in a fine-mesh strainer with the potato starch and baking powder. Sift the mixture over a sheet of wax paper.

4. In a large bowl, with an electric mixer at medium speed, beat the butter with the sugar until light and fluffy, about 3 minutes. Beat in the eggs one at a time. On low speed, stir in half of the dry ingredients. Add the rum and beat until blended. Add the remaining dry ingredients and stir just until blended. With a rubber spatula, fold in the currants.

5. Scrape the mixture into the prepared pans. Bake 1 hour or until the cakes are golden brown and a toothpick inserted in the center comes out clean.

6. Cool the cakes 10 minutes in the pans on wire racks. Invert the cakes onto the racks. Turn the cakes right side up on the racks.

Let cool completely. Serve at room temperature. Store covered with foil at room temperature up to 3 days.

Warm Amaretti Cakes

Tartine di Amaretti

Makes 6 servings

Sauris in Friuli–Venezia Giulia is a town best known for its smoked meats, such as prosciutto and speck, smoked cured ham. I will always remember it for the wonderful meal I enjoyed at Ristorante alla Pace. The dessert consisted of these warm little cakes. Serve with whipped cream or ice cream.

22 amaretti cookies

15 vanilla wafers

2 large egg yolks

$1/3$ cup heavy or whipping cream

4 large egg whites, at room temperature

Pinch of salt

Confectioner's sugar

Whipped cream or vanilla ice cream, optional

1. Place the rack to the center of the oven. Preheat the oven to 350°F.

2. Generously butter six 6-ounce timbales, ramekins, or custard cups. Place a folded kitchen towel inside a roasting pan large enough to hold the ramekins. Place the pan in the oven. Pour hot water into the pan to a depth of 1/2 inch.

3. Place the amaretti cookies in a large heavy plastic bag. Seal the bag and lightly crush the cookies with a rolling pin or other heavy object. You should have about 1 cup minus 2 tablespoons of crumbs. Repeat with the vanilla wafers in another bag. There should be 1/2 cup of these crumbs.

4. In a large bowl, stir together the egg yolks and cream. Add the crumbs and stir until moistened.

5. In a large bowl with an electric mixer, beat the egg whites on medium speed with a pinch of salt until foamy, about 1 minute. Increase the speed to high and continue beating until the whites are glossy and form soft peaks when the beaters are lifted. With a rubber spatula, gently fold a spoonful of the whites into the crumb mixture to lighten it. Fold in the remaining whites.

6. Scrape the batter into the prepared cups. Carefully place the cups on the folded towel in the pan in the oven, leaving an inch or two of space between them.

7. Bake 50 minutes or until the cakes are golden brown and a toothpick inserted in the center comes out clean.

8. Remove the cups from the pan and cool 10 minutes on a wire rack. Run a thin metal spatula around the cakes and unmold them onto serving plates. Sprinkle with confectioner's sugar. Serve warm.

Marsala Walnut Cake

Torta di Noci al Marsala

Makes 8 to 10 servings

Marsala wine gives a distinctive flavor to this cake. I like to serve it with softly whipped cream.

1¼ cups all-purpose flour

2 teaspoons baking powder

Pinch of salt

3 large eggs

1 cup sugar

⅓ cup olive oil

⅓ cup dry Marsala

1 cup walnut pieces, toasted and finely chopped (see How To Toast and Skin Nuts)

1. Place the rack in the center of the oven. Preheat the oven to 350°F. Grease a 9 × 2–inch round baking pan.

2. In a bowl, stir together the flour, baking powder, and salt.

3. In a large bowl, with an electric mixer on medium speed, beat the eggs until foamy, about 1 minute. Gradually add the sugar and continue beating until thick and pale yellow. Beat in the oil and Marsala. Fold in the dry ingredients until blended. Stir in the walnuts.

4. Scrape the batter into the prepared pan. Bake 40 minutes or until the cake is golden brown and a toothpick inserted in the center comes out clean.

5. Cool the cake in the pan on a wire rack 10 minutes. Invert the cake onto a cooling rack and let cool completely. Sprinkle with confectioner's sugar before serving. Store covered with an inverted bowl at room temperature up to 3 days.

Crunchy Walnut Cake

Torta Croccante

Makes 8 servings

This simple cake is like a giant shortbread cookie. It is crumbly, so don't try to cut it with a knife before serving. Just break it into pieces at the table.

¾ cup sugar

1 cup chopped walnuts

1 cup (2 sticks) unsalted butter, at room temperature

1 teaspoon salt

2 cups all-purpose flour

1. Place the rack in the center of the oven. Preheat the oven to 350°F. Line the bottom and sides of a 9-inch round cake pan with aluminum foil. Grease the foil.

2. Sprinkle ¼ cup of the sugar and ½ cup of the walnuts over the bottom of the prepared pan.

3. In a large bowl, with an electric mixer on medium speed, beat the butter, the remaining $1/2$ cup of sugar, and the salt until light and fluffy. On low speed, stir in the flour just until blended.

4. Crumble the dough and scatter half of the dough over the walnuts in the prepared pan. Press it into an even layer. Sprinkle with the remaining nuts. Scatter the remaining dough over the walnuts and press it into an even layer.

5. Bake for 45 minutes or until the top of the cake is firm when pressed and lightly browned.

6. Let cool for 10 minutes in the pan. Invert the cake onto a rack and carefully lift off the foil. Let cool completely. Store covered with an inverted bowl at room temperature up to 3 days.

Piedmontese Hazelnut Cake

Torta di Nocciole

Makes 8 servings

This cake is practically all nuts and butter. I like to serve it as they do in Piedmont, with a generous spoonful of warm zabaglione, but it is also good plain or with chocolate sauce and ice cream.

1½ cups toasted and skinned hazelnuts (see How To Toast and Skin Nuts)

½ cup all-purpose flour

½ teaspoon baking powder

½ teaspoon salt

½ cup (1 stick) unsalted butter

⅔ cup sugar

3 large eggs, at room temperature

Confectioner's sugar

1. Place the rack in the center of the oven. Preheat the oven to 350°F. Grease a 9 × 2-inch round baking pan.

2. In a food processor or blender, finely chop the nuts. Add the flour, baking powder, and salt and pulse just to blend.

3. In a large bowl, with an electric mixer on medium speed, beat the butter until softened. Gradually add the sugar and beat until light and fluffy, about 3 minutes. Scrape the sides of the bowl. Add the eggs one at a time, beating well after each addition. Stir in the nut mixture just until blended.

4. Spread the batter in the prepared pan. Bake 30 minutes or until the cake golden brown and a toothpick inserted in the center comes out clean.

5. Let cool 5 minutes in the pan. Invert the cake onto a cooling rack. Turn the cake right-side up onto another rack and cool completely.

6. Sprinkle with confectioner's sugar. Store covered with an inverted bowl at room temperature up to 3 days.

Mantua Cake

Torta Sbricciolona

Makes 12 servings

From Mantua, Rigoletto's hometown, comes this crumbly cake made with nuts and corn meal. It has the texture of a large crumbly cookie and should be broken rather than cut.

1 cup (2 sticks) unsalted butter, at room temperature

1 cup sugar

½ teaspoon salt

1 large egg

2 teaspoons grated lemon zest

1 teaspoon pure vanilla extract

2 cups all-purpose flour

½ cup fine yellow cornmeal

1½ cups almonds, finely chopped

Confectioner's sugar

1. Place a rack in the center of the oven. Preheat the oven to 350°F. Grease a 12 × 1–inch round pizza pan or a large baking sheet.

2. In a large bowl, beat the butter with the sugar and salt until light and fluffy. Beat in the egg, lemon zest, and vanilla. Stir in the flour, cornmeal, and nuts just until blended.

3. Scatter the dough in the prepared pan. Pat the dough out into a 12-inch circle. Bake for 30 minutes or until the center feels firm when touched and the cake is golden brown.

4. Cool 5 minutes in the pan on a wire rack. Slide a metal spatula under the cake and transfer it to a rack to cool completely

5. Sprinkle with confectioner's sugar before serving. Store covered with foil at room temperature up to 3 days.

Christmas Sweet Bread

Panettone

Makes 8 to 10 servings

At one time a specialty of northern Italy, panettone is now eaten all over Italy throughout the Christmas season, from morning breakfast with coffee to dessert with a glass of sweet wine. Visitors often bring this tall, fragrant, raisin- and candied-fruit-studded bread as a gift, so there is always plenty of it around. Leftover panettone is good toasted and spread with butter or mascarpone, or it can be mixed with other ingredients to make Panettone Bread Pudding.

½ cup milk

½ cup sugar

6 tablespoons unsalted butter

2 packages (5 teaspoons) active dry yeast or instant yeast

½ cup warm water (100° to 110°F.)

2 large eggs

2 large egg yolks

¾ cup finely chopped candied citron

½ cup currants or raisins

½ cup finely chopped candied orange peel

1 teaspoon grated lemon zest

5½ cups all-purpose flour

1. In a small saucepan, heat the milk until small bubbles form around the edges of the pan. Remove from the heat. Add the sugar and butter and let stand, stirring occasionally, until the sugar is dissolved and the mixture has cooled to lukewarm.

2. In a large electric mixer bowl, sprinkle the yeast over the warm water. Let stand until creamy, about 1 minute, then stir until the yeast is dissolved. Add the milk mixture, eggs, and yolks and beat at low speed until blended. Stir in the citron, raisins, orange peel, and lemon zest. Add the flour and beat until a stiff dough forms, about 2 minutes.

3. Scrape the dough into a large buttered bowl and turn it once to grease the top. Cover with a towel and let rise in a warm place until doubled in bulk, about 1½ hours.

4. Grease a 9 × 4–inch springform pan. (If your pan is less than 4 inches deep, make a collar for the pan: Tear off a 3-foot length of aluminum foil, and fold it in half lengthwise. Grease one side of the foil, and wrap it around the outside of the pan, greased side in. The foil will be 6 inches high. Tie kitchen string around the pan to secure the foil.)

5. Press the dough down to eliminate air bubbles. Place the dough in the prepared pan, cover with a towel, and let rise until doubled, about 1 hour.

6. Place the oven rack in the lower third of the oven. Preheat the oven to 350°F.

7. With a sharp knife, slash a cross in the top of the dough. Bake 1 hour, or until the cake is golden brown on top and a toothpick inserted in the center comes out clean.

8. Cool the cake in the pan on a rack 10 minutes. Invert the cake onto the rack, then turn it right-side up onto another rack. Let cool completely. Store covered with an inverted bowl at room temperature up to 3 days.

Chocolate-Raisin Bread Pudding

Torta di Pane Raffermo

Makes 8 servings

Italian cooks never waste bread. Leftover pieces are toasted and used as croutons or ground into crumbs. They are added to soups, torn up for meat loaves and meat balls, and even used in desserts. Bread puddings like this one are popular with home cooks. Serve it with warm Zabaglione or Warm Chocolate Sauce.

1½ cups dark raisins

⅓ cup dark rum or cognac

4 cups cubed Italian or French bread

½ cup sugar

1 quart milk

3 large eggs

½ cup unsweetened cocoa powder

⅓ cup chocolate or vanilla cookie crumbs

3 ounces semisweet or bittersweet chocolate, coarsely chopped

1. In a small bowl, soak the raisins in the rum for 1 hour.

2. Combine the bread, sugar, and milk in a large bowl. Let stand for 1 hour until the bread is very soft.

3. Place a rack in the center of the oven. Preheat the oven to 400°F. Grease a 13 × 9 × 2–inch baking dish.

4. In a large bowl, beat the eggs and cocoa. Stir the mixture into the soaked bread along with the cookie crumbs and half the chocolate.

5. Scrape the mixture into the prepared pan. Smooth the top and sprinkle with the remaining chocolate. Bake 40 minutes or until a knife inserted 1 inch from the edge of the pudding comes out clean.

6. Serve warm. Store covered with plastic wrap in the refrigerator up to 3 days.

Panettone Bread Pudding

Torta di Panettone

Makes 8 servings

Leftover sweet bread such as panettone or stollen is the traditional base for this bread pudding, but brioche or white bread can also be used.

2 cups milk

¾ cup sugar

1 cup heavy cream

¼ cup orange liqueur

¼ cup rum

3 large eggs

2 teaspoons grated orange zest

½ teaspoon ground cinnamon

8 to 12 (½-inch-thick) slices leftover homemade or store-bought panettone

⅔ cup raisins

1. Bring the milk and sugar to a simmer in a small saucepan. Stir until the sugar is dissolved, about 1 minute. Remove from the heat. Stir in the cream, orange liqueur, and rum.

2. Whisk together the eggs, zest, and cinnamon. Stir in the milk mixture.

3. Grease a 13 × 9 × 2-inch baking dish. Layer half the bread slices in the pan. Scatter the raisins on top. Arrange the remaining bread slices in the pan. Carefully pour the milk mixture over the bread slices, pressing the bread down to keep it submerged. Let stand 10 minutes until the liquid is absorbed.

4. Place a rack in the center of the oven. Preheat the oven to 375°F. Bake the pudding 40 minutes or until a knife inserted near the center comes out clean and the top is golden.

5. Cool on a wire rack. Serve warm or cool, sprinkled with confectioner's sugar. Store covered with plastic wrap in the refrigerator up to 3 days.

Biscotti Bread Pudding

Miascia

Makes 8 to 10 servings

Dry cookie and cake crumbs can be put to good use in this dessert, created by a thrifty housewife. It is so good no one will guess it was made from leftovers. Serve it slightly warm or at room temperature. Dress it up with a fruit sauce, whipped cream, or ice cream.

6 cups cubed Italian or French bread or brioche

3 cups coarsely chopped or crushed biscotti or other cookies

6 cups milk

4 large eggs

1 cup sugar

¾ cup raisins

4 ounces bittersweet or semisweet chocolate, chopped or chocolate chips

2 tablespoons slivered almonds

Confectioner's sugar

1. In a large bowl, combine the bread, cookie crumbs, and milk. Let stand for 1 hour or until the milk is absorbed.

2. Place a rack in the center of the oven. Preheat the oven to 375°F. Grease a 13 × 9 × 2–inch baking dish.

3. Beat together the eggs and sugar. Stir the egg mixture, raisins, and chocolate into the soaked bread. Spread the mixture in the prepared pan. Scatter the almonds over the top. Bake 1 hour or until the top is golden brown and a knife inserted 2 inches from the edge of the dish comes out clean.

4. Serve warm or cool, sprinkled with confectioner's sugar. Store covered with plastic wrap in the refrigerator up to 3 days.

Pear and Apple Cake

Torta di Pere e Mele

Makes 8 servings

More like a moist bread pudding than a cake, this is the perfect dessert after a winter meal. Serve it warm or chilled with whipped cream or ice cream, or with a glass of dessert wine.

Half of a small Italian or French bread loaf, cut into 1-inch cubes (about 2 cups)

2 cups milk

4 tablespoons unsalted butter

2 medium pears, such as Bartlett or Anjou, peeled, cored, and thinly sliced

2 medium apples, such as golden delicious or mutsu, peeled, cored, and thinly sliced

1 cup sugar

3 large eggs

1 teaspoon grated lemon zest

½ teaspoon ground cinnamon

½ cup golden raisins

1. In a large bowl, combine the bread and milk. Let stand until the liquid is absorbed.

2. Melt the butter in a medium saucepan over medium heat. Add the pears, apples, and sugar. Cover and cook, stirring occasionally, for 10 minutes. If there is a lot of liquid in the pan, uncover it. Cook until the fruit is very soft and the juices are thickened, about 10 to 15 minutes more.

3. Place a rack in the center of the oven. Preheat the oven to 400°F. Butter a 9-inch square baking dish.

4. Beat the eggs, lemon zest, and cinnamon. Stir the mixture into the soaked bread. Add the cooked fruits and raisins and stir well. Pour the mixture into the prepared pan and smooth the top. Bake 40 to 45 minutes or until the top is golden brown and a toothpick inserted in the center comes out clean.

5. Serve warm or at room temperature. Store covered with plastic wrap in the refrigerator up to 3 days.

Single-Crust Pastry

Pasta Frolla

Makes one 9- to 10-inch tart shell

A teaspoon of freshly grated lemon or orange zest is commonly added to this pastry for extra flavor.

1½ cups all-purpose flour

¼ cup sugar

½ teaspoon salt

8 tablespoons (1 stick) cold unsalted butter, cut into bits

2 tablespoons cold vegetable shortening

1 large egg yolk

1 teaspoon pure vanilla extract

3 to 4 tablespoons ice water

1. In a large bowl, stir together the flour, sugar, and salt.

2. Cut the butter into small pieces. Add the butter and shortening to the flour mixture. With a pastry blender or fork, blend the butter and shortening into the flour until the mixture resembles small crumbs.

3. In a small bowl, beat together the egg yolk, vanilla, and 3 tablespoons of the water. Pour the mixture over the flour and stir with a fork. Scoop up some of the mixture with your hand and rapidly squeeze it until it holds together. Repeat with the rest of the dough until the ingredients hold together and can be formed into a ball. If the mixture seems too dry and crumbly, add a teaspoon or so of cold water. Gather the dough into a disk. Wrap it in plastic wrap. Refrigerate 1 hour up to overnight.

Double-Crust Pastry

Pasta Frolla

Makes enough dough for 1 double-crust or lattice-top 9- to 10-inch tart

2½ cups all-purpose flour

⅓ cup sugar

½ teaspoon salt

12 tablespoons (1½ sticks) cold unsalted butter, cut into bits

2 tablespoons cold vegetable shortening

1 large egg yolk

1 teaspoon pure vanilla extract

3 to 4 tablespoons ice water

1. In a large bowl, stir together the flour, sugar, and salt.

2. Add the butter and shortening to the flour mixture. With a pastry blender or fork, blend the butter and shortening into the flour until the mixture resembles small crumbs.

3. In a small bowl, beat together the egg yolk, vanilla, and 3 tablespoons of the water. Pour the mixture over the flour and stir with a fork. Scoop up some of the mixture with your hand and rapidly squeeze it until it holds together. Repeat with the rest of the dough until the ingredients hold together and can be formed into a ball. If the mixture seems too dry and crumbly, add a teaspoon or so of cold water. Gather the dough into two disks, one twice as large as the other. Wrap each disk in plastic wrap. Refrigerate 1 hour up to overnight.

Berry Mascarpone Tart

Crostata di Frutti di Bosco

Makes 8 servings

Thick, rich mascarpone makes an easy filling for fruit tarts. It varies in density, so whisk in a little cream to make it light and spreadable. Pile an assortment of your favorite fresh berries on top of the cream.

1 recipe Single-Crust Pastry

8 ounces (1 cup) mascarpone

2 tablespoons sugar

½ teaspoon grated lemon zest

About ¼ cup heavy cream

1 pint raspberries

½ pint blackberries

Glaze

½ cup seedless raspberry or red current jam

2 tablespoons sugar

1. Prepare the pastry, if necessary. Then, let the dough soften briefly at room temperature. Place the dough between 2 sheets of plastic wrap and roll it out to form a 12-inch circle, about $1/8$-inch thick.

2. When the dough is ready, remove the top sheet of plastic wrap. Using the remaining sheet to lift the dough, center the dough in a 9- to 10- inch tart pan, with the plastic-covered side up. Peel off the plastic wrap. Gently press the dough into the base of the pan and along the sides. Roll the rolling pin over the top of the pan and trim off the overhanging dough. Press the dough against the sides of the pan to create a rim higher than the edge of the pan. Refrigerate the pastry shell 30 minutes.

3. Place the oven rack in the lower third of the oven. Preheat the oven to 400°F. With a fork, prick the bottom of the tart shell at 1-inch intervals. Bake 5 minutes, then prick the dough again. Bake 20 minutes more or until lightly browned and crisp.

4. Place the tart shell on a rack to cool completely. Remove the pan rim and place the tart on a serving dish.

5. In a medium bowl, combine the mascarpone, sugar, lemon zest, and enough cream to make the mixture spreadable. Spoon the

mixture into the baked tart shell and spread it evenly. Pile the berries on top.

6. Prepare the glaze: In a small saucepan, combine the jam and the sugar and bring to a simmer over medium heat. Cook until slightly thickened, 3 to 5 minutes. Brush the glaze over the berries. Serve the tart within 2 hours.

Summer Fruit Tart

Crostata di Albicocche

Makes 8 servings

Apricots, peaches, nectarines, plums, or figs can be used for this simple tart, which is perfect with ice cream or whipped cream.

- 1 recipe Single-Crust Pastry

10 to 12 ripe apricots

¼ cup plus 2 tablespoons sugar

¼ cup apricot jam

1 tablespoon rum or orange juice

Confectioner's sugar

1. Prepare the pastry, if necessary. Then, let the dough soften briefly at room temperature. Place the dough between two sheets of plastic wrap and roll it out to form a 12-inch circle, about $1/8$ inch thick.

2. When the dough is ready, remove the top sheet of plastic wrap. Using the remaining sheet to lift the dough, center the dough in a

9- to 10-inch tart pan, with the plastic-covered side up. Peel off the plastic wrap. Gently press the dough into the base of the pan and along the sides. Roll the rolling pin over the top of the pan and trim off the overhanging dough. Gently press the dough against the sides of the pan to create a rim higher than the edge of the pan. Refrigerate the pastry shell 30 minutes.

3. Place the oven rack in the lower third of the oven. Preheat the oven to 400°F.

4. Following the line around the apricots, cut them in half. Discard the pits and cut the halves into quarters. Place the quartered apricots in the pastry shell cut-side up, in concentric circles. Sprinkle with $1/4$ cup of sugar. Bake 40 to 45 minutes or until the apricots are tender and the pastry is golden brown.

5. Cool the tart in the pan on a wire cooling rack 10 minutes. Remove the pan rim and let the tart cool completely

6. In a small saucepan, heat the jam, the remaining 2 tablespoons sugar, and the rum over medium heat. Cook, stirring, until the jam is melted. Brush the glaze over the apricots. Serve within 2 hours. Just before serving, sprinkle with confectioner's sugar.

Blueberry Crostata

Crostata di Mirtille

Makes 8 servings

Blueberries are not as common as other berries in Italy. Because my husband loves blueberries, and fruit crostate, I came up with this recipe, which combines fresh and cooked berries.

1 recipe Single-Crust Pastry for a 9- or 10-inch tart pan

5 cups blueberries, rinsed and dried

$\frac{1}{3}$ cup sugar

1 tablespoon lemon juice

2 tablespoons cornstarch

2 tablespoons water

Confectioner's sugar

1. **Prepare the pastry, if necessary.** Let the dough soften briefly at room temperature. Place the dough between two sheets of plastic wrap and roll it out to form a 12-inch circle, about $1/8$-inch thick.

2. When the dough is ready, remove the top sheet of plastic wrap. Using the remaining sheet to lift the dough, center the dough in a 9- to 10-inch tart pan with the plastic-covered side up. Peel off the plastic wrap. Gently press the dough into the base of the pan and along the sides. Roll the rolling pin over the top of the pan and trim off the overhanging dough. Gently press the dough against the sides of the pan to create a rim higher than the edge of the pan. Refrigerate the pastry shell 30 minutes.

3. Place the rack in the lowest third of the oven. Preheat the oven to 400°F. With a fork, prick the bottom of the tart shell at 1-inch intervals. Bake 5 minutes, then prick the dough again. Bake 20 minutes more or until the tart shell is lightly browned and crisp.

4. Place the tart shell in the pan on a rack and cool 10 minutes. Remove the pan rim and cool completely. Place the tart shell on a serving dish.

5. To make the filling, in a medium saucepan, stir together 2 cups of the blueberries, the sugar, and the lemon juice. Bring to a simmer over very low heat. Cook until the blueberries release their juices. In a small bowl, mix together the cornstarch and 2 tablespoons of water. Pour the mixture into the simmering blueberries and cook, stirring constantly, until the mixture is thick and the juices are clear, about 1 minute. Remove from the

heat and stir in 1 cup of the remaining blueberries. (If using frozen berries, stir the remaining 3 cups into the cooked berries.)

6. Spread the blueberry mixture in the prepared tart shell. Top with the remaining fresh berries. Let cool completely. Just before serving, sprinkle with confectioner's sugar. Serve within 2 hours.

Raspberry Cream Tart

Crostata di Lampone

Makes 8 servings

This is a more elaborate tart than the Berry Mascarpone Tart. It consists of a crust that is prebaked, a creamy custard filling, and a fresh raspberry topping with a brilliant raspberry glaze. The crust can be baked and the filling made and chilled up to a day ahead. Assemble the tart up to 2 hours before serving. Store it in the refrigerator until ready to serve.

1 recipe Single-Crust Pastry

2 large egg yolks

½ cup sugar

3 tablespoons all-purpose flour

¼ teaspoon salt

1 cup milk

2 tablespoons orange liqueur

1 teaspoon pure vanilla extract

1 pint raspberries

Glaze

⅓ cup red currant jam

2 tablespoons sugar

1. Prepare the pastry, if necessary. Let the dough soften briefly at room temperature. Place the dough between two sheets of plastic wrap and roll it out to form a 12-inch circle, about $1/8$ inch thick.

2. When the dough is ready, remove the top sheet of plastic wrap. Using the remaining sheet to lift the dough, center the dough in a 9- to 10-inch tart pan with the plastic-covered side up. Peel off the plastic wrap. Gently press the dough into the base of the pan and along the sides. Roll the rolling pin over the top of the pan and trim off the overhang. Press the dough against the sides of the pan to create a rim higher than the edge of the pan. Refrigerate the pastry shell 30 minutes.

3. Place the rack in the lower third of the oven. Preheat the oven to 400°F. With a fork, prick the bottom of the tart shell at 1-inch intervals. Bake 5 minutes, then prick the dough again. Bake 20 minutes more or until the tart shell is lightly browned and crisp.

4. Let the tart shell cool completely. Remove the pan rim and place the tart shell on a serving dish.

5. To make the filling, whisk the egg yolks and sugar in a large bowl until blended. Beat in the flour and salt just until smooth.

6. In a medium saucepan, heat the milk until small bubbles form around the edges. Gradually whisk the hot milk into the egg yolks. Pour the mixture into the saucepan and cook over low heat, stirring constantly, until it comes to a boil. Lower the heat and cook 2 minutes more.

7. Pour the mixture into a bowl and stir in the orange liqueur and vanilla. Place a piece of plastic wrap directly on the surface to prevent a skin from forming. Refrigerate until chilled, at least 1 hour.

8. Pour the mixture into the pastry shell. Arrange the berries on top.

9. Prepare the glaze: Combine the jam and sugar in a small saucepan. Bring to a simmer over medium heat. Cook until thickened, about 4 minutes. Brush the glaze over the berries. Chill the tart and serve within 2 hours.

Sour-Cherry Jam Tart

Crostata di Marmellata

Makes 8 servings

Romans make this lattice-top tart with tangy sour-cherry jam. Other flavors can be used, and I have even judiciously combined a few half-empty jars of preserves with great success.

- 1 recipe Double-Crust Pastry

1½ cups sour-cherry jam

1 egg yolk beaten with 1 teaspoon water

Confectioner's sugar

1. Prepare the pastry, if necessary. Then, let the dough soften briefly at room temperature. Place the larger disk of dough between two sheets of plastic wrap and roll it out to form a 12-inch circle, about $1/8$ inch thick.

2. When the dough is ready, remove the top sheet of plastic wrap. Using the remaining sheet to lift the dough, center the dough in a 9- to 10-inch tart pan, with the plastic-covered side up. Peel off the plastic wrap. Gently press the dough into the base of the pan

and along the sides. Roll the rolling pin over the top of the pan and trim off the overhang. Press the dough against the sides of the pan to create a rim higher than the edge of the pan. Refrigerate the pastry shell 30 minutes.

3. Place the rack in the lower third of the oven. Preheat the oven to 400°F.

4. Spread the jam in the bottom of the prepared shell. Roll out the remaining dough to a 10-inch circle about $1/8$ inch thick. With a fluted pastry cutter, cut the dough into $1/2$-inch-wide strips. Arrange the strips about 1 inch apart across the jam. Rotate the tart a quarter-turn and place the remaining strips across the top, forming a lattice pattern. Press the ends of the strips against the sides of the tart to seal, and trim off the overhang. Brush the dough with the egg yolk.

5. Bake 35 to 40 minutes or until the pastry is golden brown. Let cool on a wire rack 10 minutes. Remove the pan rim and let the tart cool completely. Sprinkle with confectioner's sugar before serving. Store covered with a large inverted bowl at room temperature up to 24 hours.

Apple Marzipan Tart

Crostata di Mele

Makes 8 servings

I like to use golden delicious apples to make this beautiful tart, because they are sweet and hold their shape when baked. Another firm baking apple can be substituted.

The lattice topping on this crostata is unusual. It is made with almond paste that is piped on top of the apples. If you don't have a pastry bag, a heavy-duty plastic bag can be used.

1 recipe Single-Crust Pastry

Topping

8 ounces almond paste

1 tablespoon unsalted butter, softened

1 large egg

1 teaspoon pure vanilla extract

1 teaspoon grated lemon zest

¼ cup all-purpose flour

Filling

3 large golden delicious apples (about 1½ pounds), peeled and cut into thin slices

1 cup sugar

½ cup golden raisins

3 tablespoons amaretti cookie crumbs or plain dry bread crumbs

1 teaspoon ground cinnamon

2 tablespoons fresh lemon juice or to taste

1 large egg yolk beaten with 1 teaspoon water

Confectioner's sugar

1. Prepare the pastry, if necessary. Let the dough soften briefly at room temperature. Place the dough between two sheets of plastic wrap and roll it out to form a 12-inch circle, about $1/8$ inch thick.

2. When the dough is ready, remove the top sheet of plastic wrap. Using the remaining sheet to lift the dough, center the dough in a 9- to 10-inch tart pan, with the plastic-covered side up. Peel off

the plastic wrap. Gently press the dough into the base of the pan and along the sides. Roll the rolling pin over the top of the pan and trim off the overhanging dough. Gently press the dough against the sides of the pan to create a rim higher than the edge of the pan. Refrigerate the pastry shell 30 minutes.

3. Prepare the topping: Crumble the almond paste into a food processor or electric mixer bowl. Add the butter, egg, vanilla, and lemon zest and blend or beat until smooth. Add the flour and stir just until blended. Scoop the almond paste mixture into a pastry bag fitted with a $1/2$-inch tip.

4. Place the oven rack in the center of the oven. Preheat the oven to 400°F.

5. Combine all of the apple filling ingredients in a large bowl and stir well. Scrape the apple mixture into the prepared tart shell, packing it down lightly.

6. Pipe a circle of almond paste mixture just inside the rim of the pastry shell, being careful not to let it touch the pan, or it will stick. Pipe the remainder in a lattice pattern over the filling. Brush the egg yolk mixture over the lattice topping.

7. Place a baking sheet on the rack below the tart to catch drips. Bake the tart 1 hour 15 minutes, or until the topping is browned

and the apple juices are bubbling. If the topping browns too rapidly, cover loosely with foil.

8. Cool the tart on a rack 10 minutes. Remove the pan rim and let the tart cool completely. Serve at room temperature sprinkled with confectioner's sugar. Store covered with a large inverted bowl at room temperature up to 24 hours.

Fig and Walnut Crostata

Crostata di Fichi e Noci

Makes 8 servings

For this Piedmontese crostata, fresh figs in a creamy custard are baked in a walnut crust.

Because figs do not ripen once they are picked, look for fully matured fruits. The best are soft, with a honeylike drop of nectar visible in the small opening at the base. If ripe figs are not available, try this tart with halved apricots or sliced peaches.

Because this pastry is slightly softer than some other doughs, I like to bake the tart shell lined with buttered aluminum foil to help it hold its shape as it is baking.

1 ⅓ cups all-purpose flour

⅓ cup sugar

⅓ cup walnuts, toasted and finely ground

½ teaspoon salt

½ cup (1 stick) unsalted butter, cut into small bits

1 large egg, lightly beaten

½ teaspoon pure vanilla extract

Filling

3 tablespoons sugar

1 tablespoon flour

½ cup heavy cream

1 large egg, lightly beaten

½ teaspoon pure vanilla extract

12 to 15 ripe figs

Confectioner's sugar

1. In a large bowl, stir together the flour, sugar, walnuts, and salt. With a pastry blender or a fork, blend in the butter until the mixture resembles coarse meal. In a small bowl, beat together the egg and vanilla. Pour the egg mixture over the dry ingredients and stir with a fork. Scoop up some of the mixture with your hand and rapidly squeeze it until it holds together. Repeat with the rest of the mixture until it can be formed into a ball. If the mixture seems too dry and crumbly, add a teaspoon or so of cold water. Gather the dough into a disk. Wrap it in plastic wrap. Refrigerate 1 hour up to overnight.

2. Let the dough soften briefly at room temperature. Place the dough between two sheets of plastic wrap and roll it out to form a 12-inch circle, about $1/8$ inch thick.

3. When the dough is ready, remove the top sheet of plastic wrap. Using the remaining sheet to lift the dough, center the dough in a 9- to 10-inch tart pan, with the plastic-covered side up. Peel off the plastic wrap. Gently press the dough into the base of the pan and along the sides. Roll the rolling pin over the top of the pan and trim off the overhanging dough. Gently press the dough against the sides of the pan to create a rim higher than the edge of the pan. Refrigerate the pastry shell 30 minutes.

4. Place the rack in the lowest third of the oven. Preheat the oven to 450°F. Butter a sheet of aluminum foil. Fit the foil buttered-side down against the pastry. Bake the shell on the lowest rack of the oven 20 to 25 minutes or until lightly golden.

5. While the shell is baking, prepare the filling. In a large bowl, mix together the sugar and flour. Stir in the cream, egg, and vanilla until smooth.

6. Remove the stems of the figs and cut them in half from stem end to blossom end.

7. Remove the tart shell from the oven and place it on a cooling rack. Reduce the oven heat to 375°F. Remove the foil. If the pastry has puffed up, flatten it gently with spoon. Arrange the fig halves cut-side up in the shell. Whisk the cream filling again and drizzle it over the figs.

8. Place the tart in the oven and bake 50 minutes or until the cream is set.

9. Cool the tart on a wire rack 10 minutes Remove the pan rim and let cool completely. Dust with confectioner's sugar before serving. Store covered with a large inverted bowl at room temperature up to 24 hours.

Dried Fig Tart

Crostata di Fichi

Makes 8 servings

The fresh fig season is short, but sweet dried figs are available all year. For this tart, the figs are cooked into a thick, jamlike puree and sandwiched between two layers of tender pastry.

- 1 recipe Double-Crust Pastry dough

1 pound dried figs, stemmed and coarsely chopped

¼ cup sugar

½ cup fresh orange juice

¾ cup water

½ teaspoon grated orange zest

1 egg yolk beaten with 1 teaspoon water, for glaze

Confectioner's sugar

1. Prepare the pastry, if necessary. Let the larger piece of dough soften briefly at room temperature. Place the dough between

two sheets of plastic wrap and roll it out to form a 12-inch circle, about $1/8$ inch thick.

2. When the dough is ready, remove the top sheet of plastic wrap. Using the remaining sheet to lift the dough, center the dough in a 9- to 10-inch tart pan, with the plastic-covered side up. Peel off the plastic wrap. Gently press the dough into the base of the pan and along the sides. Roll the rolling pin over the top of the pan and trim off the overhanging dough. Gently press the dough against the sides of the pan to create a rim higher than the edge of the pan. Refrigerate the pastry shell 30 minutes.

3. In a medium saucepan, combine the figs, sugar, juice, and water. Bring to a simmer over medium heat. Cook, stirring occasionally, until thick, about 10 minutes. Let cool 30 minutes. Stir in the zest.

4. Place the oven rack on the lowest level. Preheat the oven to 350°F. Spread the fig mixture in the bottom of the prepared shell.

5. Roll out the remaining dough to a 10-inch circle about $1/8$ inch thick. With a fluted pastry wheel, cut the dough into $1/2$-inch-wide strips. Arrange the strips about 1 inch apart across the jam. Rotate the tart a quarter-turn and place the remaining strips

across the top, forming a lattice pattern. Press the ends of the strips against the sides of the tart to seal. Brush the dough with the egg yolk.

6. Bake 35 to 40 minutes or until the pastry is golden brown.

7. Let the tart cool in the pan on a wire rack 10 minutes. Remove the pan rim and let the tart cool completely. Sprinkle with confectioner's sugar. Store covered with a large inverted bowl at room temperature up to 24 hours.

Lemon Almond Tart

Crostata di Limone e Mandorle

Makes 8 servings

This Pugliese-style tart has an almond crust and a lemon creamy filling.

Pastry

⅓ cup almonds

3 tablespoons sugar

1 cup all-purpose flour

½ teaspoon salt

6 tablespoons unsalted butter

About 3 tablespoons ice water

½ teaspoon pure vanilla extract

Filling

3 large eggs

1 cup sugar

½ cup fresh lemon juice

1 tablespoon grated lemon zest

4 tablespoons unsalted butter, melted and cooled

1. Prepare the pastry: Place the almonds and sugar in a food processor or blender. Process or blend until the nuts are very finely chopped.

2. Transfer the almond mixture to a large bowl. Stir in the flour and salt. With a pastry blender, cut in the butter until the mixture resembles coarse crumbs. Drizzle with 3 tablespoons of the water and toss until the dough begins to hold together and form a dough. Add a little more water if necessary. Transfer the dough to a sheet of plastic wrap and press it together to form a disk. Wrap and refrigerate 1 hour up to overnight.

3. Let the dough soften briefly at room temperature. Place the dough between two sheets of plastic wrap and roll it out to form a 12-inch circle, about $1/8$ inch thick.

4. When the dough is ready, remove the top sheet of plastic wrap. Using the remaining sheet to lift the dough, center the dough in a 9- to 10-inch tart pan, with the plastic-covered side up. Peel off

the plastic wrap. Gently press the dough into the base of the pan and along the sides. Roll the rolling pin over the top of the pan and trim off the overhanging dough. Gently press the dough against the sides of the pan to create a rim higher than the edge of the pan. Refrigerate the pastry shell 30 minutes.

5. Place the oven rack in the lowest third of the oven. Preheat the oven to 425°F. With a fork, prick the bottom of the tart shell at 1-inch intervals. Bake the pastry 5 minutes. Prick the shell again. Bake 20 minutes more or until the tart shell is lightly browned and crisp. Remove the tart shell from the oven and place it on a wire rack. Reduce the heat to 325°F.

6. Prepare the filling: Whisk the eggs, sugar, lemon juice, and zest in a large bowl. Whisk in the butter.

7. Pour the filling into the crust. Bake the tart 20 minutes or until the filling is set but still slightly soft in the center.

8. Cool the tart 10 minutes in the pan on a wire rack. Remove the rim of the pan and let the tart cool completely on the rack. Transfer the tart to a serving platter. Serve at room temperature. Store covered with a large inverted bowl in the refrigerator up to 24 hours.

Almond and Peach Tart

Crostata di Mandorle

Makes 8 servings

Almond paste and thick peach preserves make a memorable filling combination in this rich tart.

    1 recipe Single-Crust Pastry

3 large eggs, at room temperature

¼ cup sugar

8 ounces almond paste

½ cup all-purpose flour

¾ cup peach or apricot jam

½ cup sliced almonds

Confectioner's sugar

1. Prepare the pastry, if necessary. Let the dough soften briefly at room temperature. Place the dough between two sheets of plastic wrap and roll it out to form a 12-inch circle, about ⅛ inch thick.

2. When the dough is ready, remove the top sheet of plastic wrap. Using the remaining sheet to lift the dough, center the dough in a 9- to 10-inch tart pan, with the plastic-covered side up. Peel off the plastic wrap. Gently press the dough into the base of a 9- to 10-inch tart pan and along the sides. Roll the rolling pin over the top of the pan and trim off the overhanging dough. Gently press the dough against the sides of the pan to create a rim higher than the edge of the pan. Refrigerate the pastry shell 30 minutes.

3. Place an oven rack on the lowest level. Preheat the oven to 350°F.

4. In a large bowl, with an electric mixer, beat the eggs until foamy. Gradually beat in the sugar. Crumble the almond paste into the egg mixture and beat until smooth, about 4 minutes. Fold in the flour.

5. Spread the jam over the bottom of the prepared shell. Spread the almond paste mixture over the jam. Sprinkle with the sliced almonds.

6. Bake 30 to 35 minutes, or until the filling is puffed and golden.

7. Let the tart cool in the pan on a wire rack 10 minutes. Remove the pan rim and let the tart cool completely. Just before serving, sprinkle with confectioner's sugar. Serve at room temperature.

Store covered with an inverted bowl in the refrigerator up to 24 hours.

Pine Nut Tart

Crostata di Pinoli

Makes 8 servings

Pine nuts, tender seeds extracted from pinecones, are used in many desserts and savory dishes throughout Italy. Buy them in bulk at health food stores or ethnic markets rather than in those expensive little jars at the supermarket. If you prefer, slivered almonds can be substituted for the pine nuts.

1 recipe Single-Crust Pastry

½ cup apricot or peach jam

2 large eggs, separated

½ cup sugar

1 teaspoon pure vanilla extract

Pinch of salt

1 cup toasted pine nuts

Confectioner's sugar

1. Prepare the pastry, if necessary. Let the dough soften briefly at room temperature. Place the dough between two sheets of plastic wrap and roll it out to form a 12-inch circle, about $1/8$ inch thick.

2. When the dough is ready, remove the top sheet of plastic wrap. Using the remaining sheet to lift the dough, center the dough in a 9- to 10-inch tart pan, with the plastic-covered side up. Peel off the plastic wrap. Gently press the dough into the base of the pan and along the sides. Roll the rolling pin over the top of the pan and trim off the overhanging dough. Gently press the dough against the sides of the pan to create a rim higher than the edge of the pan. Refrigerate the pastry shell 30 minutes.

3. Place an oven rack on the lowest level. Preheat the oven to 350°F.

4. Spread the jam over the bottom of the prepared pastry.

5. In a large bowl, with an electric mixer on medium speed, whisk the egg yolks, sugar, and vanilla until fluffy and pale yellow, about 4 minutes.

6. In a large clean bowl with clean beaters, beat the egg whites with the salt on low speed until foamy. Increase the speed to high and beat until the egg whites hold soft peaks when the

beaters are lifted, about 4 minutes. Fold the whites into the yolk mixture. Gently fold in the pine nuts. Scrape the mixture into the tart shell.

7. Bake 35 to 40 minutes or until the tart is puffed and golden.

8. Let the tart cool in the pan on a wire rack 10 minutes. Remove the pan rim and let the tart cool completely. Sprinkle with confectioner's sugar before serving. Store covered with an inverted bowl in the refrigerator up to 24 hours.

Winter Fruit and Nut Crostata

Crostata di Inverno

Makes 8 servings

Dried fruits and nuts have a rich flavor that is a welcome complement to winter meals.

    1 recipe Double-Crust Pastry

1 (12-ounce) box pitted dried plums (prunes)

1 cup dark raisins

1 cup water

1 teaspoon grated orange zest

¼ cup orange liqueur or rum

2 tablespoons honey

½ teaspoon ground cinnamon

1 cup toasted walnuts, chopped (see How To Toast and Skin Nuts)

1 egg yolk beaten with 1 teaspoon water

Confectioner's sugar

1. Prepare the pastry, if necessary. Let the dough soften briefly at room temperature. Place the larger disk of dough between two sheets of plastic wrap and roll it out to form a 12-inch circle, about $1/8$ inch thick.

2. When the dough is ready, remove the top sheet of plastic wrap. Using the remaining sheet to lift the dough, center the dough in a 9- to 10-inch tart pan, with the plastic-covered side up. Peel off the plastic wrap. Gently press the dough into the base of the pan and along the sides. Roll the rolling pin over the top of the pan and trim off the overhanging dough. Gently press the dough against the sides of the pan to create a rim higher than the edge of the pan. Refrigerate the pastry shell 30 minutes.

3. In a medium saucepan, combine the prunes, raisins, and water. Cook over low heat until soft, about 10 minutes. Let cool. In a food processor or blender, puree the fruit mixture with the orange zest. Add the liqueur, honey, and cinnamon and process until smooth. With a spatula, stir in the walnuts.

4. Spread the fruit and nut mixture in the prepared tart shell.

5. Place an oven rack in the lower third of the oven. Preheat the oven to 350°F.

6. Roll out the remaining dough to a 10-inch circle. With a fluted pastry wheel, cut the dough into $1/2$-inch-wide strips. Arrange the strips about 1 inch apart across the tart pan. Rotate the tart a quarter-turn and place the remaining strips across the top, forming a lattice pattern. Press the ends of the strips against the sides of the tart to seal. Brush the dough with the egg yolk mixture.

7. Bake 35 to 40 minutes, or until the pastry is golden brown.

8. Let the tart cool in the pan on a wire rack 10 minutes. Remove the pan rim and let the tart cool completely. Sprinkle with confectioner's sugar. Store covered with a large inverted bowl at room temperature up to 24 hours.

Ricotta Lattice Tart

Crostata di Ricotta

Makes 8 servings

Tarts and cakes made with ricotta are popular all over southern Italy. There are infinite variations.

> 1 recipe Double-Crust Pastry Dough

½ cup dark raisins

2 tablespoons orange liqueur or rum

16 ounces whole or part-skim ricotta

2 large eggs

½ cup sugar

1 teaspoon pure vanilla extract

1 egg yolk beaten with 1 teaspoon water

Confectioner's sugar

1. Prepare the pastry, if necessary. Let the dough soften briefly at room temperature. Place the larger piece of dough between two sheets of plastic wrap and roll it out to form a 12-inch circle, about $1/8$ inch thick.

2. When the dough is ready, remove the top sheet of plastic wrap. Using the remaining sheet to lift the dough, center the dough in a 9- to 10-inch tart pan, with the plastic-covered side up. Peel off the plastic wrap. Gently press the dough into the base of the pan and along the sides. Roll the rolling pin over the top of the pan and trim off the overhanging dough. Gently press the dough against the sides of the pan to create a rim higher than the edge of the pan. Refrigerate the pastry shell 30 minutes.

3. In a small bowl, toss the raisins with the liqueur. Let stand 30 minutes.

4. In a large bowl, beat together the ricotta, eggs, sugar, and vanilla until well blended. Stir in the raisins and liqueur. Scrape the filling into the prepared pastry shell.

5. Place the oven rack in the lowest third of the oven. Preheat the oven to 350°F. Roll out the remaining piece of pastry to a 10-inch circle about $1/8$ inch thick. With a fluted pastry wheel, cut the dough into $1/2$-inch-wide strips. Arrange half the strips about 1 inch apart over the filling. Rotate the tart a quarter-turn and arrange the remaining strips over the tart, forming a lattice

pattern. Press the ends of the strips against the sides of the tart shell to seal. Lightly brush the dough strips with the egg wash.

6. Bake 50 minutes, or until the filling is puffed and the pastry is golden brown.

7. Let cool in the pan on a wire rack 10 minutes. Remove the rim of the pan and transfer the tart to a serving platter. Store covered with a large inverted bowl in the refrigerator up to 24 hours.

Roman Ricotta Tart

Pizza Dolce di Ricotta

Makes 8 servings

Almost as flat as a pizza, this ricotta tart is my version of one from the popular Forno, a bakery in Rome's Campo dei Fiori. Customers line up for slices of fresh-baked pizza bianca, olive bread, and simple sweets like this tart. Though they are always busy, the good-natured staff makes sure that everyone's cravings are satisfied.

This tart is a little more rustic than the others and is made with a dough that is patted out, rather than rolled. The dough is made with baking powder, so it puffs up slightly as it bakes.

Pastry

1½ cups all-purpose flour

⅓ cup sugar

½ teaspoon salt

½ teaspoon baking powder

6 tablespoons (¾ stick) chilled unsalted butter, cut into bits

2 tablespoons solid vegetable shortening

1 large egg, lightly beaten

Filling

1 (3-ounce) package cream cheese, softened

¼ cup sugar

1 tablespoon dark rum

1 large egg yolk

1 cup (8 ounces) whole or part-skim ricotta

1. Prepare the pastry: In a large bowl, combine the flour, sugar, salt, and baking powder.

2. Add the butter and shortening to the flour mixture. With a pastry blender or a fork, cut in the butter until the mixture resembles small crumbs. Stir in the egg until a soft dough forms. Scoop up some of the mixture with your hand and rapidly squeeze it until it holds together. Repeat with the rest of the dough until it can be formed into a ball. If the mixture seems too dry and crumbly, add a teaspoon or so of cold water. Pat the dough into the bottom and against the sides of a 9- to 10-inch tart pan with a removable bottom. Refrigerate 30 minutes.

3. Place the oven rack in the lower third of the oven. Preheat the oven to 350°F. Prepare the filling: In a large bowl, beat together the cream cheese, sugar, and rum. Beat in the egg yolk until well blended. Add the ricotta and beat until smooth.

4. Spread the mixture in the prepared tart shell. Bake 45 minutes or until puffed and golden brown.

5. Cool the tart in the pan on a wire rack 10 minutes. Remove the pan rim and let the tart cool completely. Serve at room temperature or refrigerate about 1 hour and serve slightly chilled. Store covered with an inverted bowl in the refrigerator up to 24 hours.

Ricotta Jam Tart

Crostata di Ricotta e Marmellata

Makes 8 servings

I like to use apricot jam for this tart, but fruit flavors such as raspberry or orange marmalade would be good too.

1 recipe Single-Crust Pastry

Filling

1½ cups (12 ounces) whole or part-skim ricotta

2 large eggs

¼ cup sugar

1 teaspoon pure vanilla extract

1 cup best-quality apricot jam

1. Prepare the pastry, if necessary. Let the dough soften briefly at room temperature. Place the dough between two sheets of plastic wrap and roll it out to form a 12-inch circle, about ⅛ inch thick.

2. When the dough is ready, remove the top sheet of plastic wrap. Using the remaining sheet to lift the dough, center the dough in a 9- to 10-inch tart pan, with the plastic-covered side up. Peel off the plastic wrap. Gently press the dough into the base of the pan and along the sides. Roll the rolling pin over the top of the pan and trim off the overhanging dough. Gently press the dough against the sides of the pan to create a rim higher than the edge of the pan. Refrigerate the pastry shell 30 minutes.

3. Place an oven rack in the lowest third of the oven. Preheat the oven to 350°F.

4. Prepare the filling: In a large bowl, whisk together the ricotta, eggs, sugar, and vanilla until well blended.

5. Spread the jam in the prepared tart shell. Pour the ricotta mixture over the jam and spread it evenly.

6. Bake 55 to 60 minutes or until puffed and golden.

7. Let the tart cool in the pan on a wire rack 10 minutes. Remove the pan rim and let the tart cool completely. Serve at room temperature or refrigerate about 1 hour and serve slightly chilled. Store covered with an inverted bowl in the refrigerator up to 24 hours.

Chocolate Tart

Crostata di Cioccolata

Makes 8 servings

Trieste is a cosmopolitan city that has at different times belonged to both Austria and Italy. True to its Austrian roots, it has many old-world coffee houses serving a range of pastries that you will not find anywhere else in Italy. At one, I had a memorable tart filled with lush chocolate cream, like the inside of a truffle. This is my version of that rich tart.

    1 recipe Single-Crust Pastry

Filling

1 cup heavy cream

8 ounces bittersweet chocolate, broken into small pieces

½ teaspoon instant espresso powder

1. Prepare the pastry, if necessary. Let the dough soften briefly at room temperature. Place the dough between two sheets of plastic wrap and roll it out to form a 12-inch circle, about $1/8$-inch thick.

2. When the dough is ready, remove the top sheet of plastic wrap. Using the remaining sheet to lift the dough, center the dough a 9- to 10-inch tart pan, with the plastic-covered side up. Peel off the plastic wrap. Gently press the dough into the base of the pan and along the sides. Roll the rolling pin over the top of the pan and trim off the overhanging dough. Gently press the dough against the side of the pan to create a rim higher than the edge of the pan. Refrigerate the pastry shell 30 minutes.

3. Place an oven rack in the lowest third of the oven. Preheat the oven to 450°F. With a fork, prick the bottom of the tart shell at 1-inch intervals. Bake 5 minutes, then prick the dough again. Bake 20 minutes more or until lightly browned and crisp.

4. Place the tart shell on a rack to cool. Remove the pan rim and place the tart on a serving dish.

5. To make the filling, place the cream in a small heavy saucepan. Bring the cream to a simmer and remove from the heat. Add the chocolate and espresso powder. Let stand several minutes or until the chocolate is softened. Stir the filling until smooth.

6. Pour the chocolate into the cooled tart shell. Refrigerate 4 hours up to overnight. Serve chilled.

Rice Pudding Tart

Crostata di Riso

Makes 8 servings

In Parma, miniature versions of this comforting tart are served with midmorning coffee. I like it best when it is still slightly warm.

3 cups whole milk

¼ cup medium-grain rice, such as Arborio, Carnaroli, or Vialone Nano

½ cup sugar

2 tablespoons unsalted butter

1 recipe Single-Crust Pastry

2 large eggs

1 teaspoon grated lemon zest

2 tablespoons finely chopped candied orange peel or citron

2 tablespoons golden raisins

1. In a medium saucepan, bring the milk to a simmer. Add the rice, sugar, and butter and cook over low heat, stirring occasionally, until the rice is very tender, about 30 minutes. Transfer to a bowl and let cool about 30 minutes, stirring occasionally.

2. Prepare the pastry, if necessary. Let the dough soften briefly at room temperature. Place the dough between two sheets of plastic wrap and roll it out to form a 12-inch circle, about $1/8$ inch thick.

3. When the dough is ready, remove the top sheet of plastic wrap. Using the remaining sheet to lift the dough, center the dough in a 9- to 10- inch tart pan, with the plastic-covered side up. Peel off the plastic wrap. Gently press the dough into the base of the pan and along the sides. Roll the rolling pin over the top of the pan and trim off the overhanging dough. Gently press the dough against the sides of the pan to create a rim higher than the edge of the pan. Refrigerate the pastry shell 30 minutes.

4. Place an oven rack on the lowest level. Preheat the oven to 350° F.

5. In a medium bowl, beat the eggs and lemon zest. Stir into the cooled rice mixture. Stir in the orange peel and raisins. Scrape the mixture into the prepared shell.

6. Bake 40 to 45 minutes or until the filling is just set.

7. Let the tart cool in the pan on a wire rack 10 minutes. Remove the pan rim and let the tart cool 1 hour. Store covered with an inverted bowl in the refrigerator up to 24 hours.

Cornmeal Berry Tart

Crostata di Mirtilli e Lampone

Makes 8 servings

Cornmeal adds a pleasant crunch and golden color to the crust for this tart I had in Tuscany. The dough is crumbly, so it is easier to pat it into the pan than to roll it out. The lattice topping is made by rolling pieces of the dough into long ropes. The filling is a tart-sweet mix of fresh berries—I like to use blueberries and raspberries, but others can be substituted.

Filling

2 cups blueberries

1 cup raspberries

1 cup sugar

1/8 teaspoon ground cinnamon

Pastry

2 cups all-purpose flour

1/3 cup yellow cornmeal

½ cup sugar

1 teaspoon baking powder

1 teaspoon grated lemon zest

½ teaspoon salt

¾ cup (1½ sticks) chilled unsalted butter, cut into bits

3 large egg yolks

3 to 4 tablespoons ice water

Confectioner's sugar

1. Prepare the filling: In a medium saucepan, combine the berries, sugar, and cinnamon. Cover and bring to a simmer over medium heat. Uncover and cook, stirring occasionally, until the mixture has thickened, about 20 minutes. Transfer to a bowl and let cool, then cover and chill in the refrigerator 1 hour up to overnight. The mixture will thicken further as it cools.

2. Prepare the crust: In a large bowl, combine the flour, cornmeal, sugar, lemon zest, baking powder, and salt. With a pastry blender or a fork, cut in the butter until the mixture resembles coarse crumbs. Beat 2 of the egg yolks together with 3 tablespoons of the water. Drizzle the mixture over the dough

and stir lightly into the flour mixture until it begins to form a dough.

3. Scoop up a handful of the dough and squeeze it together. Continue squeezing the dough by handfuls until the dough can be formed into a ball. Add the remaining 1 tablespoon of water if needed.

4. Place the oven rack in the lowest third of the oven. Preheat the oven to 350°F. Scatter about two-thirds of the crust mixture over the bottom of a 9-inch tart pan with a removable bottom. Press the crumbs evenly over the bottom and up the sides of the pan to form a pastry shell. Spoon the chilled blueberry mixture into the shell and smooth the top.

5. On a lightly floured surface, roll the remaining crust mixture with your hands into $1/2$-inch-thick ropes. Arrange the ropes 1 inch apart across the filling. Rotate the tart a quarter-turn and place the remaining strips across the top, forming a lattice pattern. Press the ends of the strips against the sides of the tart to seal, and trim off the overhang. Brush the dough with the remaining egg yolk.

6. Bake the tart 45 to 50 minutes, or until golden brown.

7. Let the tart cool in the pan on a wire rack 10 minutes. Remove the rim of the pan and let the tart cool completely. Just before serving, sprinkle with confectioner's sugar. Store covered with an inverted bowl at room temperature up to 24 hours.

Spice and Nut Tart

Crostata allo Spezie

Makes 8 servings

This tart from the Alto Adige area is something like a Linzer tart. Serve it in small slices at teatime.

2½ cups all-purpose flour

1 teaspoon baking powder

1 teaspoon ground cinnamon

½ teaspoon ground cloves

½ teaspoon salt

1 cup ground toasted walnuts (see How To Toast and Skin Nuts)

½ cup (1 stick) cold unsalted butter, cut into bits

1 cup sugar

2 large eggs

1 teaspoon grated lemon zest

1 cup blackberry or raspberry jam

Confectioner's sugar

1. In a large bowl, stir together the flour, baking powder, cinnamon, cloves, and salt. Stir in the walnuts.

2. In another large bowl, using an electric mixer, beat the butter with the sugar until light and fluffy, about 2 minutes. Add the eggs one at a time, beating well after each addition. Beat in the lemon zest. Add the dry ingredients and stir on low speed until blended, about 2 minutes more. Divide the dough into 2 disks, one twice as large as the other. Wrap each disk in plastic wrap and refrigerate 1 hour up to overnight.

3. Let the dough soften briefly at room temperature. Place the largest ball of dough between two sheets of plastic wrap and roll it out to form a 12-inch circle, about $1/8$ inch thick.

4. When the dough is ready, remove the top sheet of plastic wrap. Using the remaining sheet to lift the dough, center the dough in a 9- to 10-inch tart pan, with the plastic-covered side up. Peel off the plastic wrap. Gently press the dough into the base of the pan and along the sides. Roll the rolling pin over the top of the pan and trim off the overhanging dough. Gently press the dough against the sides of the pan to create a rim higher than the edge of the pan. Refrigerate the pastry shell 30 minutes.

5. Place the oven rack in the lowest third of the oven. Preheat the oven to 375°F.

6. Spread the jam evenly in the tart shell. Roll out the remaining dough to a 10-inch circle. Cut the dough into $1/2$-inch-wide strips. Arrange half the strips 1 inch apart across the filling. Press the ends against the sides of the tart shell to seal. Rotate the tart pan a quarter-turn and arrange the remaining strips of dough 1 inch apart across the tart to form a lattice pattern. Press the ends against the sides to seal. Trim off the excess dough.

7. Bake the tart 40 minutes or until the crust is golden brown.

8. Cool the tart in the pan on a rack 10 minutes. Remove the pan rim. Let the tart cool completely. Just before serving, sprinkle with confectioner's sugar. Store at room temperature covered with a large inverted bowl up to 24 hours.

Cinnamon Plum Torte

Torta di Susine

Makes 8 servings

Deeper than a tart, this fruit-filled torte is baked in a springform pan.

3 cups all-purpose flour

¾ cup sugar

2 teaspoons baking powder

½ teaspoon ground cinnamon

1 teaspoon salt

¾ cup (1½ sticks) unsalted butter, at room temperature

1 large egg

1 large egg yolk

1 teaspoon grated lemon zest

1 teaspoon pure vanilla extract

Filling

2½ pounds firm ripe prune plums, thinly sliced

½ cup sugar

½ teaspoon ground cinnamon

1 tablespoon fresh lemon juice

1 tablespoon unsalted butter, cut into bits

1 large egg yolk, lightly beaten

Confectioner's sugar

1. In a large bowl, stir together the flour, sugar, baking powder, cinnamon, and salt. Cut the butter into small pieces. With a pastry blender, cut in the butter until the mixture resembles coarse crumbs. In a small bowl, beat the whole egg, egg yolk, lemon zest, and vanilla. Stir into the flour mixture until a dough forms. Add a little ice water if the dough seems dry.

2. Divide the dough into two pieces, one twice as large as the other. Shape each piece into a flat disk. Wrap each one in plastic wrap and chill for at least 1 hour or overnight.

3. Let the dough soften briefly at room temperature. Place the larger portion of dough between two sheets of plastic wrap and roll it out to form a 12-inch circle, about $1/8$ inch thick.

4. When the dough is ready, remove the top sheet of plastic wrap. Using the remaining sheet to lift the dough, center the dough in a 9- to 10-inch tart pan, with the plastic-covered side up. Peel off the plastic wrap. Gently press the dough into the base of the pan and along the sides. Roll the rolling pin over the top of the pan and trim off the overhanging dough. Gently press the dough against the sides of the pan to create a rim higher than the edge of the pan. Refrigerate the pastry shell 30 minutes.

5. Place the oven rack in the lowest third of the oven. Preheat the oven to 350°F.

6. Prepare the filling: In a large bowl, toss together the plums, sugar, cinnamon, and lemon juice. Spread the filling in the prepared pastry shell. Dot with the butter.

7. Roll out the remaining dough to a 10-inch circle. With a pastry cutter, cut the dough into $1/2$-inch-wide strips. Arrange half the strips 1 inch apart across the filling. Press the ends against the sides of the tart shell to seal. Rotate the tart pan a quarter-turn and place the remaining strips of dough 1 inch apart across the

tart to form a lattice pattern. Press the ends against the sides to seal. Trim off the excess dough.

8. Brush the top with the egg yolk. Bake 1 hour or until the pastry is golden brown and the juices are bubbling.

9. Transfer the pan to a cooling rack and let cool 10 minutes. Remove the rim of the pan and let the tart cool completely. Sprinkle with confectioner's sugar. Store covered with a large inverted bowl at room temperature up to 24 hours.

Cannoli Cream

Ricotta Cream

Makes about 4 cups

This cream is good not just as a filling for cannoli shells or cream puffs but also layered with fresh fruit as a spoon dessert. It can be made up to 24 hours before using.

2 pounds whole or part-skim milk ricotta, drained, if necessary (see To Drain Ricotta)

1½ cups confectioner's sugar

1 teaspoon pure vanilla extract

½ teaspoon ground cinnamon

2 ounces semisweet chocolate, chopped (optional)

2 tablespoons chopped candied orange peel or citron (optional)

1. Put the ricotta in a food processor and blend it until creamy. Add the sugar, vanilla, and cinnamon and blend until smooth. Scrape the mixture into a bowl.

2. With a spoon or spatula, stir in the chocolate and candied fruit, if using. Cover and refrigerate until ready to use.

Chocolate Cannoli Cream

Makes about 4 cups

To make black-and-white cannoli, fill one side of the cannoli tube with the vanilla filling, and the other side with this chocolate filling. This is also good as a filling for layer cake or cream puff shells.

2 pounds whole or part-skim ricotta, drained if necessary (see To Drain Ricotta)

1½ cups confectioner's sugar

½ cup unsweetened cocoa powder

1 teaspoon pure vanilla extract

In an electric mixer or food processor, combine the ricotta, sugar, cocoa, and vanilla. Mix until smooth and well blended.

Pastry Cream

Crema Pasticcieria

Makes about 5 cups

This cream is the foundation for many Italian desserts, including Italian Trifle (Zuppa Inglese). Flavor the cream with lemon or orange zest or dried or candied fruits. Use it as a filling for Cream Puffs and napoleons, serve it like pudding, or spoon it over fruit or cake. This recipe can easily be halved.

1 quart milk

½ cup sugar

6 large egg yolks

½ cup all-purpose flour

2 teaspoons pure vanilla extract

1. In a heavy saucepan, bring 3 cups of the milk and the sugar to a simmer over medium heat, stirring to dissolve the sugar. Remove from the heat.

2. In a large heatproof bowl, whisk the egg yolks and the remaining 1 cup milk until blended. Place the flour in a fine-mesh strainer. Shake it over the egg yolks. Whisk until smooth. Beat in the hot milk a little at a time.

3. When all of the milk has been added, transfer the mixture to the saucepan and return it to the heat. Cook over medium heat, stirring constantly with a wooden spoon, until the mixture begins to boil. Reduce the heat and cook 30 seconds more. Remove the pan from the heat and stir in the vanilla.

4. Transfer to a bowl. Cover with plastic wrap, pressing the plastic against the surface of the cream. Chill up to 24 hours.

Variation: *Chocolate and Vanilla Pastry Creams*: Make Pastry Cream through step 3. Divide the cream between two bowls. Add 4 ounces chopped semisweet chocolate to one bowl and let stand 1 minute until softened. Stir well. Cover both creams with plastic wrap, pressing the plastic against the surface of the cream, and chill.

Cream Puffs

Bignè

Makes 12

Though made all over Italy, bignè, or cream puffs, are a Neapolitan specialty. When I was growing up, my mother made them for every holiday. At Gambrinus, a favorite cafe near the Naples opera house, my husband and I indulged in jumbo cream puffs filled with whipped cream, the inspiration for this recipe.

The typical fillings are pastry cream and ricotta cream, but ice cream is also good. Tuscans fill small cream puffs with vanilla pastry cream, pile them on a platter, and drizzle them with chocolate sauce. They call them bongo bongo. The puffs can be baked ahead and frozen until needed. If they have been frozen, place them in a 350°F oven to crisp. Let them cool before filling them.

½ cup (1 stick) unsalted butter

1 cup water

½ teaspoon salt

1 cup all-purpose flour

4 large eggs, at room temperature

2 cups chilled heavy or whipping cream

1 teaspoon pure vanilla extract

2 tablespoons confectioner's sugar, plus more for dusting the tops

1. Place a rack in the center of the oven. Preheat the oven to 400°F. Butter and flour a large baking sheet.

2. In a medium saucepan over medium-low heat, bring the butter, water, and salt to a rapid boil. Remove from the heat. Add the flour all at once and stir well with a wooden spoon until the flour is completely incorporated and a dough has formed.

3. Return the saucepan to the stove over medium heat. Cook, stirring constantly and turning the dough often, until the dough begins to leave a thin film on the bottom of the saucepan, about 3 minutes. (This dries the dough so the cream puffs will be crisp.) With a rubber spatula, scrape the dough into a large bowl.

4. With a wooden spoon, beat in the eggs one at a time until they are thoroughly incorporated. Continue to beat until smooth and shiny, about 2 minutes.

5. Scoop up a rounded tablespoon of the dough. Use a second spoon to push the dough off the spoon onto the prepared baking sheet. Form 12 mounds, spaced about 3 inches apart. With moistened fingertips, pat the tops to round the shape.

6. Bake the cream puffs 40 to 45 minutes, until golden brown. Turn off the oven and remove the puffs. With a small knife, make a small hole in the side of each puff to allow the steam to escape. Return the puffs to the oven for 10 minutes to dry.

7. Using a serrated knife, cut the puffs partway in half horizontally. Open like a book and scoop out the soft dough from the inside. Transfer to a wire rack and let cool completely.

8. At least 20 minutes before you are ready to fill the cream puffs, place a large bowl and the beaters of an electric mixer in the refrigerator.

9. Remove the bowl and beaters. Pour the cream into the bowl. Add the vanilla and the 2 tablespoons confectioner's sugar. With the mixer, whip the cream until it holds soft peaks, about 4 minutes. Spoon the cream into the puffs. Dust with additional confectioner's sugar and serve immediately.

St. Joseph's Fritters

Sfinci di San Giuseppe

Makes 8 servings

St. Joseph is the patron saint of fathers in Sicily, and these pastries are eaten on his feast day, March 19. Though they are usually filled with ricotta cream, you can also make them with Pastry Cream.

$1/2$ recipe Cannoli Cream

Dough

1 cup water

¼ cup unsalted butter

1 teaspoon salt

1 cup all-purpose flour

4 large eggs

Vegetable oil for frying

Candied orange peel and candied cherries, for garnish

Confectioner's sugar

1. Prepare the cream, if necessary. In a medium saucepan over medium-low heat, heat the water, butter, and salt until the butter melts and the mixture reaches a boil. Remove from the heat. Add the flour all at once and stir well with a wooden spoon until the flour is completely incorporated and a dough has formed.

2. Return the saucepan to the stove over medium heat. Cook, stirring constantly and turning the dough often, until the dough begins to leave a thin film on the bottom of the saucepan, about 3 minutes. (This dries the dough so the fritters will be crisp.) With a rubber spatula, scrape the dough into a large bowl.

3. With a wooden spoon, beat in the eggs one at a time until thoroughly incorporated. Continue to beat until smooth and shiny, about 2 minutes.

4. Line a tray with paper towels. In a deep heavy saucepan or deep-fryer, heat 3 inches of oil to 370° F on a frying thermometer, or until a small bit of the dough dropped into the oil sizzles and swims rapidly around the pan and turns brown in 1 minute. Scoop up about 1 rounded tablespoon of the batter. With another spoon, push the batter into the oil, being careful not to splash it.

5. Add just enough spoonfuls of batter to the pan to fit without crowding. The batter will puff up and double or triple in size. Cook, turning the fritters often, about 4 minutes. (When they are almost done, the fritters will break open.) Continue to cook 1 to 2 minutes more or until the fritters are crisp and golden brown. Remove the fritters with a slotted spoon or skimmer. Place them on the paper towels to drain. Repeat with the remaining batter.

6. When all of the fritters have been fried, let them cool about 10 minutes. With a small knife, split the fritters partially open like a book. Fill with the cannoli cream. Garnish the cream with strips of candied orange peel and candied cherries.

7. Sprinkle with confectioner's sugar and serve warm. These are best eaten soon after they are made.

www.ingramcontent.com/pod-product-compliance
Lightning Source LLC
Chambersburg PA
CBHW071820080526
44589CB00012B/865